Enthusiasm

Unleash Your Inner Spark: Mastering the Art of Enthusiasm
to Transform Your Life and Achieve Lasting Success in
Every Area of Your Being - A Comprehensive Guide to Igniting Your Passion, Overcoming Obstacles, and Creating a
Life You Love!

Lance P. Richards

Enthusiasm: Unleash Your Inner Spark: Mastering the Art of Enthusiasm to Transform Your Life and Achieve Lasting Success in Every Area of Your Being - A Comprehensive Guide to Igniting Your Passion, Overcoming Obstacles, and Creating a Life You Love!

Table of Contents

01: Introduction: Why Enthusiasm Matters

Introduction:

Enthusiasm is an incredibly powerful force that can transform your life in profound ways. It can inspire you to take action, fuel your motivation, and help you overcome even the greatest obstacles. With enthusiasm, you can achieve lasting success in every area of your being, from your career and relationships to your physical and mental health.

But what is enthusiasm, exactly? At its core, enthusiasm is a powerful and positive emotion that arises when we are engaged in something we love or deeply care about. It is the spark that ignites our passions and drives us to pursue our dreams and goals with energy and excitement.

In this comprehensive guide to enthusiasm, we will explore the art of mastering this powerful emotion so that you can create a life you truly love. We will delve into the science behind enthusiasm and its benefits, as well as the various techniques and strategies you can use to cultivate and maintain it.

01: INTRODUCTION: WHY ENTHUSIASM MATTERS

Why Enthusiasm Matters:

Enthusiasm is an incredibly important emotion that can have a profound impact on your life. It is the force that propels you forward, motivates you to take action, and helps you overcome obstacles that might otherwise seem insurmountable. With enthusiasm, you can achieve your goals, no matter how lofty or challenging they may seem.

One of the most important benefits of enthusiasm is its impact on your mental and physical health. When you are enthusiastic about something, you feel more energized, optimistic, and positive. This can have a profound impact on your overall well-being, reducing stress and anxiety, boosting your immune system, and even helping you live longer.

Enthusiasm also plays a key role in your relationships, both personal and professional. When you approach your interactions with others with enthusiasm, you are more likely to build strong connections and inspire others to follow your lead. You will also be more resilient in the face of challenges, and better able to adapt to changing circumstances.

Finally, enthusiasm is essential for achieving success in your career. When you approach your work with passion and energy, you are more likely to excel and be recognized for your efforts. You will also be more resilient in the face of setbacks and setbacks, and better able to learn from your mistakes and move forward with confidence.

Conclusion:

Enthusiasm is a powerful force that can transform your life in countless ways. Whether you are looking to improve your mental and physical health, build stronger relationships, or achieve lasting success in your career, enthusiasm is the key to unlocking your full potential.

In this comprehensive guide to enthusiasm, we will explore the various techniques and strategies you can use to cultivate and maintain this powerful emotion. From mindfulness and gratitude to positive thinking and goal-setting, we will cover everything you need to know to unleash your inner spark and create a life you truly love.

02: Defining Enthusiasm: What It Is and What It Is Not

Defining Enthusiasm: What It Is and What It Is Not

Enthusiasm is a powerful emotion that can have a transformative effect on our lives. It is often described as a feeling of intense excitement, passion, and eagerness. When we are enthusiastic about something, we feel energized, optimistic, and engaged. It is a powerful force that can propel us forward, motivating us to take action and pursue our goals with vigor and determination.

However, while enthusiasm is often spoken of in positive terms, it is important to recognize that it is not always a force for good. In some cases, enthusiasm can be misguided, leading us to pursue goals or ideas that are ultimately harmful to ourselves or others. In this chapter, we will explore what enthusiasm is, what it is not, and how to harness its power for positive outcomes.

What is Enthusiasm?

At its core, enthusiasm is a positive emotion that arises when we are engaged in something we care deeply about. It is a feeling of excitement and eagerness that can help us overcome obstacles and achieve our goals. When we are enthusiastic, we feel a sense of purpose and motivation, and we are more likely to put in the effort required to succeed.

Enthusiasm can arise in many different contexts, from pursuing a new hobby or interest to working towards a professional goal or project. It can also arise in personal relationships, fueling our desire to connect with others and build strong, meaningful connections.

What Enthusiasm is Not

While enthusiasm is generally viewed as a positive emotion, it is important to recognize that it is not always a force for good. In some cases, enthusiasm can be misguided or misplaced, leading us to pursue goals or ideas that are ultimately harmful to ourselves or others.

One common example of misguided enthusiasm is the pursuit of fad diets or extreme exercise regimes. While it is important to prioritize our health and well-being, it is equally important to do so in a safe and sustainable way. Pursuing extreme or unhealthy habits in the name of enthusiasm can ultimately do more harm than good, leading to physical or mental health problems.

Another example of misguided enthusiasm is the pursuit of get-rich-quick schemes or other unrealistic goals. While it is important to be ambitious and pursue our dreams, it is equally important to do so in a realistic and practical way. Pursuing goals that are unlikely to succeed can ultimately lead to disappointment and frustration.

Harnessing the Power of Enthusiasm

While enthusiasm can be misguided in some cases, it is an incredibly powerful force when harnessed for positive outcomes. To do so, it is important to approach enthusiasm with a sense of mindfulness and self-awareness.

One key aspect of harnessing enthusiasm is to set realistic and achievable goals. When we are enthusiastic about a goal, it can be easy to get swept up in the excitement and lose sight of what is realistically achievable. By setting achievable goals, we can ensure that our enthusiasm is channeled in a productive and sustainable way.

02: DEFINING ENTHUSIASM: WHAT IT IS AND WHAT IT IS NOT

Another important aspect of harnessing enthusiasm is to remain mindful of our actions and their impact on others. While enthusiasm can be a powerful motivator, it is important to ensure that our enthusiasm is not causing harm to ourselves or others. By remaining mindful and aware, we can ensure that our enthusiasm is channeled in a positive and productive way.

Conclusion

Enthusiasm is a powerful force that can have a transformative effect on our lives. When harnessed for positive outcomes, enthusiasm can help us overcome obstacles and achieve our goals with vigor and determination. However, it is important to approach enthusiasm with a sense of mindfulness and self-awareness, to ensure that our enthusiasm is channeled in a productive and sustainable way. By doing so, we can unleash our inner spark and create a life we truly love.

03: The Benefits of Living with Enthusiasm

The Benefits of Living with Enthusiasm

Enthusiasm is a powerful force that can have a profound impact on our lives. When we live with enthusiasm, we approach life with a sense of passion and purpose, and we are more likely to achieve our goals and find lasting success. In this chapter, we will explore the many benefits of living with enthusiasm, and how it can help us create a life we truly love.

Increased Energy and Motivation

One of the most obvious benefits of living with enthusiasm is increased energy and motivation. When we are enthusiastic about something, we are more likely to feel energized and engaged, and we are more likely to put in the effort required to achieve our goals. This can be particularly important in areas where we might otherwise feel stuck or unmotivated, such as in our career or personal relationships.

Greater Resilience and Persistence

Another key benefit of living with enthusiasm is greater resilience and persistence. When we are enthusiastic about a goal or idea, we are more likely to persist in the face of obstacles and setbacks. This can be particularly important when pursuing long-term goals, which may require sustained effort and commitment over an extended period of time.

Improved Creativity and Problem-Solving

Living with enthusiasm can also improve our creativity and problem-solving abilities. When we approach life with a sense of passion and curiosity, we are more likely to think outside the box and come up with innovative solutions to the challenges we face. This can be particularly important in areas such as business or entrepreneurship, where creativity and innovation are key to success.

Improved Physical and Mental Health

Living with enthusiasm can also have significant benefits for our physical and mental health. When we are enthusiastic about life, we are more likely to take care of ourselves, prioritize our health and well-being, and engage in activities that bring us joy and fulfillment. This can lead to reduced stress, improved mood, and greater overall happiness and well-being.

Enhanced Relationships and Social Connections

Finally, living with enthusiasm can enhance our relationships and social connections. When we approach life with a sense of passion and positivity, we are more likely to attract others who share our energy and enthusiasm. This can lead to deeper, more meaningful relationships, and a greater sense of community and belonging.

Cultivating Enthusiasm in Our Lives

While the benefits of living with enthusiasm are clear, it can sometimes be difficult to cultivate this mindset in our lives. One key aspect of cultivating enthusiasm is to focus on the things that bring us joy and fulfillment, and to prioritize these activities in our lives. This might mean pursuing a hobby or interest that we are passionate about, or seeking out new experiences and opportunities that challenge us and push us outside our comfort zone.

Another important aspect of cultivating enthusiasm is to remain mindful and present in our lives. When we are mindful, we are more likely to appreciate the simple pleasures of life, and to approach even mundane tasks with a sense of curiosity and engagement. This can help us find joy and fulfillment in even the most ordinary aspects of our lives.

Conclusion

Living with enthusiasm can have a profound impact on our lives, leading to increased energy and motivation, greater resilience and persistence, improved creativity and problem-solving abilities, enhanced physical and mental health, and deeper relationships and social connections. By cultivating enthusiasm in our lives, we can create a life we truly love, and achieve lasting success in every area of our being.

04: How Enthusiasm Impacts Your Mental Health

Introduction

The connection between enthusiasm and mental health is a fascinating and complex topic. Enthusiasm is often thought of as a positive emotion, one that is associated with joy, excitement, and inspiration. Mental health, on the other hand, is a term that encompasses a wide range of conditions that affect a person's mood, behavior, and thoughts. In this chapter, we will explore the impact that enthusiasm can have on mental health and how cultivating enthusiasm can help individuals overcome mental health challenges.

The Power of Enthusiasm

Enthusiasm is a powerful emotion that can motivate and inspire individuals to take action towards their goals. When we are enthusiastic about something, we are filled with energy and passion, and we approach our tasks with a positive attitude. Enthusiasm is contagious, and it can spread to those around us, creating a positive and supportive environment. When we are enthusiastic about our work or our relationships, we are more likely to be successful, both professionally and personally.

Enthusiasm and Mental Health

Research has shown that enthusiasm can have a positive impact on mental health. When we are enthusiastic, we are less likely to experience negative emotions such as anxiety, depression, and stress. Enthusiasm can also help individuals cope with difficult situations, such as the loss of a loved one or a job, by providing a sense of purpose and meaning.

Studies have also found that enthusiastic individuals are more resilient in the face of adversity. They are better able to bounce back from setbacks and failures and are less likely to experience burnout. Enthusiasm can also help individuals build stronger relationships, as it fosters a sense of connection and community.

Cultivating Enthusiasm

If enthusiasm is so beneficial to mental health, how can individuals cultivate it? The first step is to identify the things that bring us joy and excitement. It could be a hobby, a career, a relationship, or a cause that we are passionate about.

Once we have identified these things, we should make time for them in our lives and prioritize them.

Another way to cultivate enthusiasm is to set goals for ourselves. Goals give us something to work towards and a sense of accomplishment when we achieve them. It is important to set realistic and achievable goals, as unrealistic goals can lead to disappointment and frustration.

Finally, cultivating a positive mindset can also help us cultivate enthusiasm. We should focus on the positive aspects of our lives and practice gratitude for the things we have. We should also surround ourselves with positive and supportive people who encourage us and inspire us.

Overcoming Mental Health Challenges with Enthusiasm

For individuals who are struggling with mental health challenges, cultivating enthusiasm can be a powerful tool in their recovery. Enthusiasm can provide a sense of purpose and meaning, and it can motivate individuals to take action towards their recovery. By focusing on the things that bring them joy and excitement, individuals can find a sense of hope and optimism that can help them overcome their challenges.

Enthusiasm can also help individuals build resilience in the face of adversity. By approaching their challenges with a positive attitude and a sense of determination, individuals can overcome even the most difficult obstacles.

Conclusion

Enthusiasm is a powerful emotion that can have a profound impact on mental health. By cultivating enthusiasm, individuals can find a sense of purpose and meaning in their lives, build resilience in the face of adversity, and create stronger relationships with those around them. Whether we are struggling with mental health challenges or simply looking to improve our overall well-being, cultivating enthusiasm is an important step towards creating a life we love.

05: How Enthusiasm Impacts Your Physical Health

Introduction

Enthusiasm is often thought of as a positive emotion, one that is associated with joy, excitement, and inspiration. In addition to its impact on mental health, enthusiasm can also have a significant impact on physical health. In this chapter, we will explore the ways in which enthusiasm can impact physical health, as well as how cultivating enthusiasm can help individuals improve their overall well-being.

The Connection Between Enthusiasm and Physical Health

Research has shown that there is a strong connection between enthusiasm and physical health. Enthusiasm can lead to a variety of physical health benefits, including:

– Reduced Stress: When we are enthusiastic, we are less likely to experience negative emotions such as anxiety, depression, and stress. Lower levels of stress can lead to improved immune function, lower blood pressure, and a reduced risk of chronic diseases such as heart disease and diabetes.

05: HOW ENTHUSIASM IMPACTS YOUR PHYSICAL HEALTH

– Increased Energy: Enthusiasm is associated with increased energy levels, which can lead to improved physical performance and a greater sense of vitality.

– Improved Sleep: When we are enthusiastic, we are more likely to feel fulfilled and content, which can lead to improved sleep quality and duration.

– Stronger Immune System: Enthusiasm can also have a positive impact on the immune system, by reducing stress and increasing the production of antibodies.

Cultivating Enthusiasm for Physical Health

Cultivating enthusiasm can be a powerful tool for improving physical health. Here are some ways to cultivate enthusiasm:

– Find Your Passion: Identify the activities or hobbies that bring you joy and excitement, and make time for them in your life. This can be anything from hiking and yoga to cooking and art.

– Set Goals: Setting goals for yourself can help you cultivate enthusiasm and motivation. Make sure your goals are realistic and achievable, and celebrate your progress along the way.

– Stay Positive: Cultivate a positive mindset by focusing on the positive aspects of your life and practicing gratitude for the things you have. Surround yourself with positive and supportive people who encourage you and inspire you.

– Exercise Regularly: Regular exercise can help boost your energy levels and improve your overall physical health. Find an exercise routine that you enjoy and make it a regular part of your daily routine.

– Take Care of Your Body: Eating a healthy diet, getting enough sleep, and reducing stress can all have a positive impact on physical health. Make sure you are taking care of your body by getting enough rest, eating nutritious foods, and finding ways to manage stress.

Conclusion

Enthusiasm is a powerful emotion that can have a significant impact on physical health. By cultivating enthusiasm, individuals can reduce stress, increase energy, improve sleep, and strengthen their immune system. By finding their passion, setting goals, staying positive, exercising regularly, and taking care of their body, individuals can harness the power of enthusiasm to improve their physical health and create a life they love.

06: How Enthusiasm Impacts Your Relationships

Introduction

Enthusiasm is a powerful emotion that can impact every area of our lives, including our relationships. When we approach our relationships with enthusiasm, we are more likely to connect deeply with others, build strong bonds, and experience greater satisfaction and happiness in our interactions. In this chapter, we will explore the ways in which enthusiasm impacts our relationships, and how we can cultivate enthusiasm to improve our connections with others.

The Importance of Enthusiasm in Relationships

Enthusiasm is essential for building and maintaining healthy, positive relationships. When we approach our relationships with enthusiasm, we are more likely to:

— Build Trust: Enthusiasm can help build trust between people by demonstrating a genuine interest in the other person and their experiences.

— Increase Intimacy: Enthusiasm can increase feelings of intimacy and emotional connection between partners, friends, and family members.

– Strengthen Communication: Enthusiasm can enhance communication skills by creating an open and positive environment for conversation and sharing.

– Improve Overall Satisfaction: Enthusiasm can improve overall relationship satisfaction by creating a sense of excitement and joy in spending time with the other person.

Cultivating Enthusiasm in Relationships

Cultivating enthusiasm in relationships can be challenging, but it is well worth the effort. Here are some ways to cultivate enthusiasm in your relationships:

– Be Present: When spending time with others, be fully present and engaged in the moment. Listen actively, ask questions, and show genuine interest in the other person and their experiences.

– Show Appreciation: Express gratitude for the people in your life and the things they do for you. Small gestures of appreciation, such as saying thank you or leaving a note, can go a long way in cultivating enthusiasm and positive feelings in relationships.

– Share Your Enthusiasm: Share your passions and interests with others. Invite them to participate in activities
that you enjoy or ask them to share their own passions and
interests.

– Communicate Effectively: Effective communication is essential for cultivating enthusiasm in relationships. Practice
active listening, use positive language, and show empathy
and understanding when communicating with others.

– Be Supportive: Show support and encouragement for the
people in your life. Celebrate their accomplishments and
provide emotional support during difficult times.

Conclusion

Enthusiasm is a key ingredient for building and maintaining
healthy, positive relationships. By approaching our relationships with enthusiasm, we can build trust, increase intimacy, improve communication, and experience greater satisfaction and happiness in our interactions. Cultivating enthusiasm in relationships requires effort and practice, but

the rewards are well worth it. By being present, showing appreciation, sharing our enthusiasm, communicating effectively, and being supportive, we can harness the power of enthusiasm to transform our relationships and create a life we love.

07: How Enthusiasm Impacts Your Career

Introduction

Enthusiasm is a powerful emotion that can have a significant impact on our careers. When we approach our work with enthusiasm, we are more likely to experience greater job satisfaction, build strong relationships with colleagues, and achieve greater success in our careers. In this chapter, we will explore the ways in which enthusiasm impacts our careers, and how we can cultivate enthusiasm to improve our professional lives.

The Importance of Enthusiasm in Your Career

Enthusiasm is a critical component of career success. When we approach our work with enthusiasm, we are more likely to:

– Improve Job Performance: Enthusiasm can improve job performance by increasing motivation, focus, and productivity. Enthusiastic individuals are more likely to take on new challenges and strive for excellence in their work.

– Increase Job Satisfaction: Enthusiasm can increase job

satisfaction by creating a sense of purpose and meaning in our work. When we are enthusiastic about our work, we are more likely to feel fulfilled and satisfied with our careers.

– Enhance Professional Relationships: Enthusiasm can enhance professional relationships by creating a positive and supportive work environment. Enthusiastic individuals are more likely to build strong relationships with colleagues and work collaboratively to achieve common goals.

– Increase Career Opportunities: Enthusiasm can open doors to new career opportunities by demonstrating a willingness to learn, take on new challenges, and strive for excellence in our work.

Cultivating Enthusiasm in Your Career

Cultivating enthusiasm in our careers can be challenging, but it is possible. Here are some ways to cultivate enthusiasm in your career:

– Find Your Passion: Identify your passions and interests and find ways to incorporate them into your work. When we are passionate about our work, we are more likely to approach it with enthusiasm and energy.

07: HOW ENTHUSIASM IMPACTS YOUR CAREER

– Set Goals: Set goals for your career and work towards achieving them. Setting goals can provide a sense of purpose and direction in our work, and help us stay motivated and focused.

– Focus on the Positive: Focus on the positive aspects of your work and look for opportunities to learn and grow. When we focus on the positive, we are more likely to approach our work with enthusiasm and energy.

– Be Proactive: Take initiative and be proactive in your work. When we take ownership of our work and take on new challenges, we are more likely to approach our work with enthusiasm and energy.

– Stay Connected: Stay connected with colleagues and build strong professional relationships. When we have positive relationships with colleagues, we are more likely to approach our work with enthusiasm and energy.

Conclusion

Enthusiasm is a critical component of career success. By approaching our work with enthusiasm, we can improve job performance, increase job satisfaction, enhance professional relationships, and increase career opportunities. Cultivating enthusiasm in our careers requires effort and practice, but the rewards are well worth it. By finding our passion, setting goals, focusing on the positive, being proactive, and staying connected, we can harness the power of enthusiasm to transform our careers and create a life we love.

08: Overcoming Obstacles to Enthusiasm

Introduction

Obstacles are a natural part of life. We all face challenges that can sap our enthusiasm and make it difficult to stay motivated and passionate about our goals. Whether it's a difficult project at work, a personal setback, or a health issue, obstacles can derail our enthusiasm and leave us feeling discouraged and disheartened. However, overcoming obstacles is essential if we want to maintain our enthusiasm and achieve lasting success in every area of our lives. In this chapter, we will explore some of the most common obstacles to enthusiasm and strategies for overcoming them.

Obstacle 1: Fear

Fear is one of the most significant obstacles to enthusiasm. Whether it's fear of failure, fear of the unknown, or fear of rejection, fear can stop us in our tracks and prevent us from pursuing our goals with passion and enthusiasm. To overcome fear, we must identify the source of our fear and challenge our limiting beliefs. We must remind ourselves that failure is a natural part of the learning process, and that success often requires taking risks and stepping outside of our comfort zones. By reframing our mindset around fear, we can overcome this obstacle and approach our goals with renewed enthusiasm and confidence.

Obstacle 2: Procrastination

Procrastination is another common obstacle to enthusiasm. When we put off tasks or delay action on our goals, we can quickly lose momentum and enthusiasm. To overcome procrastination, we must identify the root cause of our procrastination and take proactive steps to address it. This may involve breaking down tasks into smaller, more manageable steps, creating a schedule or timeline, or seeking support and accountability from others. By taking action and making progress towards our goals, we can overcome procrastination and reignite our enthusiasm.

Obstacle 3: Burnout

Burnout is a state of physical, emotional, and mental exhaustion that can occur when we push ourselves too hard and neglect self-care. Burnout can drain our enthusiasm and leave us feeling exhausted and unmotivated. To overcome burnout, we must prioritize self-care and take time to rest and recharge. This may involve taking breaks throughout the day, practicing mindfulness or meditation, engaging in hobbies or activities that bring us joy, or seeking professional support if necessary. By prioritizing self-care and addressing burnout, we can restore our energy and enthusiasm for our goals.

Obstacle 4: Negative Self-Talk

Negative self-talk is another obstacle that can drain our enthusiasm and self-confidence. When we engage in negative self-talk, we can create a self-fulfilling prophecy that reinforces our limiting beliefs and undermines our enthusiasm. To overcome negative self-talk, we must become aware of our inner dialogue and challenge our negative beliefs. We can do this by reframing our thoughts and focusing on positive self-talk and affirmations. By practicing self-compassion and reframing our mindset, we can overcome negative self-talk and approach our goals with renewed enthusiasm.

Obstacle 5: Lack of Support

Finally, a lack of support can be a significant obstacle to enthusiasm. When we lack support from others, we can feel isolated and discouraged, which can quickly drain our enthusiasm and motivation. To overcome this obstacle, we must seek out support from others who share our goals and passions. This may involve joining a support group, seeking mentorship or coaching, or simply reaching out to friends and family for support. By surrounding ourselves with a supportive network of individuals, we can overcome this obstacle and approach our goals with renewed enthusiasm and energy.

Conclusion

Obstacles are a natural part of life, but they don't have to stop us from pursuing our goals with enthusiasm and passion. By identifying the obstacles that are holding us back and taking proactive steps to overcome them, we can cultivate a mindset of resilience and perseverance that will serve us well in every area of our lives. Whether we are facing fear, procrastination, burnout, negative self-talk, or a lack of support, there are always strategies and tools we can use to overcome these obstacles and reignite our enthusiasm. It's important to remember that enthusiasm is not a constant state, and it's normal to experience ups and downs in our levels of motivation and passion. However, by developing a mindset of enthusiasm and actively working to overcome obstacles, we can create a life that is fulfilling, meaningful, and full of purpose.

Ultimately, enthusiasm is a powerful force that can transform our lives in profound ways. When we approach our goals with passion and enthusiasm, we are more likely to succeed, to overcome obstacles, and to create a life we love. By mastering the art of enthusiasm, we can unleash our inner spark and tap into our full potential, achieving lasting success in every area of our being.

09: Identifying Your Passion: What You Love and What You Don't

Passion is the driving force behind enthusiasm. When we are passionate about something, we are filled with energy, motivation, and a sense of purpose. Identifying our passions is essential to unleashing our inner spark and creating a life we love. In this chapter, we will explore how to identify our passions by examining what we love and what we don't.

What You Love

One of the most effective ways to identify your passions is to think about what you love. What activities or hobbies bring you joy? What topics or subjects fascinate you? What do you find yourself daydreaming about or losing track of time while doing? These are all clues to your passions.

Start by making a list of all the things you love to do, even if they seem unrelated or insignificant. Don't worry about whether they are practical or whether you can make a career out of them. Just focus on what brings you joy and fulfillment. Once you have a list, try to identify any common themes or patterns. Are there certain skills or interests that appear repeatedly? This can help you pinpoint your passions.

It's important to remember that passions can evolve and change over time. What you loved as a child may not be the same as what you love now. So, keep an open mind and be willing to explore new interests and experiences.

What You Don't Love

Another way to identify your passions is to examine what you don't love. Sometimes, it's easier to know what we don't want than what we do want. Ask yourself: What activities or situations drain your energy or leave you feeling unfulfilled? What tasks or responsibilities do you dread? What do you find yourself avoiding or procrastinating on?

Making a list of what you don't love can help you identify the areas of your life that are not aligned with your passions. It can also help you recognize patterns or themes that may be holding you back. For example, if you find that you don't enjoy working in a fast-paced environment, it may be a sign that you are better suited for a more relaxed, creative setting.

09: IDENTIFYING YOUR PASSION: WHAT YOU LOVE AND WHAT YOU DON'T

Sometimes, we may be unsure about what we don't love because we haven't tried it yet. In this case, it's important to be willing to experiment and try new things. Don't be afraid to step outside of your comfort zone and explore new experiences. You may discover a new passion that you never knew existed.

The Intersection of Love and Don't Love

Once you have identified what you love and what you don't love, it's time to explore the intersection between the two. Are there any activities or interests that you love, but also find challenging or difficult? These are the areas where you may have the potential to grow and develop your passions even further.

It's also important to consider how your passions align with your values and goals. For example, if you are passionate about helping others, you may want to explore careers in social work or non-profit organizations. If you are passionate about the environment, you may want to explore careers in sustainability or conservation.

Ultimately, identifying your passions is an ongoing process.

09: IDENTIFYING YOUR PASSION: WHAT YOU LOVE AND WHAT YOU DON'T

It requires self-reflection, experimentation, and a willingness to explore new experiences. By understanding what you love and what you don't love, you can begin to unleash your inner spark and create a life that is filled with enthusiasm, purpose, and fulfillment.

10: Cultivating a Growth Mindset for Enthusiasm

Introduction:

Your mindset can have a significant impact on your ability to cultivate enthusiasm and pursue your passions. A growth mindset is the belief that your abilities and intelligence can be developed through hard work, dedication, and learning from your failures. In contrast, a fixed mindset is the belief that your abilities and intelligence are predetermined and cannot be changed. In this chapter, we will explore the importance of cultivating a growth mindset for enthusiasm and how to develop this mindset.

The Importance of a Growth Mindset for Enthusiasm:

Having a growth mindset is essential for cultivating enthusiasm because it allows you to see challenges and failures as opportunities for growth and learning. Instead of being discouraged by setbacks, you can use them as a chance to improve and develop new skills. When you approach challenges with a growth mindset, you are more likely to persevere and maintain your enthusiasm for your goals.

10: CULTIVATING A GROWTH MINDSET FOR ENTHUSIASM

Developing a Growth Mindset:

– Embrace Challenges:

To develop a growth mindset, it's essential to embrace challenges and view them as opportunities for growth. Instead of avoiding difficult tasks, embrace them as a chance to learn and develop new skills. Set challenging goals for yourself, and when you encounter obstacles, use them as opportunities to learn and grow.

– Learn from Failure:

Another crucial aspect of a growth mindset is learning from failure. Instead of being discouraged by setbacks, view them as opportunities to learn and improve. Analyze what went wrong and identify what you can do differently in the future. Failure is an inevitable part of the learning process, and a growth mindset enables you to use failure as a stepping stone to success.

– Practice Self-Reflection:

Self-reflection is an important tool for cultivating a growth mindset. Regularly take time to reflect on your successes and failures and identify areas where you can improve. Consider what strategies worked well and what didn't and use this information to adjust your approach moving forward. By reflecting on your experiences, you can learn from them and continue to grow.

– Emphasize Effort over Talent:

A growth mindset emphasizes effort over innate talent. Instead of believing that you have a predetermined level of talent, focus on putting in the effort to develop your skills. Recognize that progress takes time and effort, and with persistence, you can achieve your goals.

– Surround Yourself with Positive Influences:

Surrounding yourself with positive influences can help you maintain a growth mindset. Seek out people who are enthusiastic, supportive, and encouraging. Engage in conversations with people who inspire you and share your passion. By surrounding yourself with positive influences, you can reinforce your growth mindset and maintain your enthusiasm for your goals.

10: CULTIVATING A GROWTH MINDSET FOR ENTHUSI-ASM

Conclusion:

Developing a growth mindset is essential for cultivating enthusiasm and pursuing your passions. By embracing challenges, learning from failure, practicing self-reflection, emphasizing effort over talent, and surrounding yourself with positive influences, you can develop a growth mindset that enables you to persevere in the face of obstacles and maintain your enthusiasm for your goals.

11: How to Practice Mindfulness to Boost Enthusiasm

In today's fast-paced world, it's easy to get lost in the hustle and bustle of everyday life. We're constantly bombarded with information, distractions, and stressors that can drain our energy and make it difficult to stay enthusiastic about our goals and passions. That's why practicing mindfulness can be a powerful tool for boosting enthusiasm and finding greater meaning and purpose in life.

Mindfulness is the practice of being fully present and aware of the present moment, without judgment. It's about paying attention to your thoughts, feelings, and sensations in a non-judgmental way, and learning to observe them without getting caught up in them. By cultivating mindfulness, you can learn to stay centered, focused, and energized, even in the midst of challenging circumstances.

Here are some tips on how to practice mindfulness to boost enthusiasm:

– Set aside time for mindfulness meditation

One of the most effective ways to cultivate mindfulness is

through regular meditation practice. Meditation can help you quiet your mind and develop greater focus and awareness. Set aside a few minutes each day to sit quietly, close your eyes, and focus on your breath. When your mind wanders, gently bring it back to your breath. Over time, you'll find that you're able to stay more present and focused throughout the day.

– Practice mindful breathing

Even if you don't have time for a formal meditation practice, you can still cultivate mindfulness by paying attention to your breath throughout the day. Take a few deep, slow breaths and notice the sensation of the air moving in and out of your body. Whenever you feel stressed or overwhelmed, take a few moments to focus on your breath and bring yourself back to the present moment.

– Practice mindful eating

Mindful eating is a simple practice that can help you develop greater awareness and appreciation for your food. Before you eat, take a moment to pause and notice the colors, textures, and smells of your food. Take a few slow, deliberate bites, and pay attention to the sensations in your mouth and the flavors in your food. By practicing mindful eating, you can learn to savor your food more fully and develop a greater sense of gratitude for the nourishment it provides.

– Practice mindful movement

Mindful movement practices like yoga, tai chi, or qigong can help you cultivate mindfulness while also improving your physical health and flexibility. These practices involve slow, deliberate movements that are synchronized with the breath, helping to quiet the mind and bring you into a state of focused awareness.

– Practice gratitude

Gratitude is a powerful tool for cultivating enthusiasm and positivity. Take a few minutes each day to reflect on the things you're grateful for, whether it's your health, your relationships, your job, or your hobbies. By focusing on the positive aspects of your life, you can cultivate a greater sense of enthusiasm and motivation for pursuing your goals and passions.

11: HOW TO PRACTICE MINDFULNESS TO BOOST EN-THUSIASM

In conclusion, mindfulness is a powerful tool for boosting enthusiasm and finding greater meaning and purpose in life. By practicing mindfulness regularly, you can learn to stay centered, focused, and energized, even in the midst of challenging circumstances. Whether through meditation, mindful breathing, mindful eating, or mindful movement, there are many ways to cultivate mindfulness and experience the many benefits it has to offer. So why not give it a try and see how it can transform your life?

12: The Role of Gratitude in Fostering Enthusiasm

Gratitude is a powerful emotion that can transform the way we see ourselves and the world around us. It is the feeling of appreciation for what we have, rather than focusing on what we lack. By practicing gratitude, we can shift our perspective and develop a more positive outlook on life. Gratitude can play a crucial role in fostering enthusiasm and helping us to live a more fulfilling life.

One of the benefits of practicing gratitude is that it helps us to focus on the present moment. When we feel grateful for what we have, we are less likely to worry about the future or dwell on the past. This can be especially helpful for those who struggle with anxiety or depression. By focusing on the present moment, we can cultivate a sense of peace and calm that can help us to feel more enthusiastic about life.

Another way that gratitude can boost enthusiasm is by helping us to recognize the good things in our lives. When we take the time to appreciate what we have, we are more likely to feel satisfied and content with our lives. This can help us to cultivate a sense of joy and excitement that can fuel our enthusiasm for the future.

12: THE ROLE OF GRATITUDE IN FOSTERING ENTHU-SIASM

Gratitude can also help us to develop a more positive mindset. When we practice gratitude, we are more likely to focus on the positive aspects of our lives, rather than dwelling on the negative. This can help us to cultivate a sense of optimism and hope that can be a powerful force for change.

One way to practice gratitude is to keep a gratitude journal. Each day, write down three things that you are grateful for. These can be big or small things, such as the sunshine, a good meal, or a kind word from a friend. By focusing on the positive aspects of your life, you can cultivate a sense of gratitude that can help to boost your enthusiasm and sense of well-being.

Another way to practice gratitude is to take the time to thank those around you. Whether it's thanking a friend for their support or expressing gratitude to a coworker for their hard work, taking the time to appreciate others can help us to cultivate a sense of gratitude and connection.

In addition to these practices, there are many other ways that you can cultivate gratitude in your life. Some people find that meditation or mindfulness practices can help them to develop a greater sense of gratitude. Others may find that engaging in acts of service or volunteer work can help them to feel more grateful for what they have. Whatever method you choose, the key is to make gratitude a regular part of your life.

In conclusion, cultivating gratitude is an essential part of fostering enthusiasm and living a more fulfilling life. By focusing on the positive aspects of our lives and expressing gratitude for what we have, we can shift our perspective and develop a more positive mindset. This can help us to cultivate a sense of joy and excitement that can fuel our enthusiasm and help us to achieve our goals. So take the time to cultivate gratitude in your life and see how it can transform your outlook and your sense of well-being.

13: Finding Inspiration to Fuel Your Enthusiasm

Introduction:

Inspiration is a powerful force that can fuel our enthusiasm and ignite our inner spark. It is what motivates us to take action, pursue our dreams, and achieve our goals. However, finding inspiration is not always easy, especially when we face challenges, setbacks, and obstacles along the way. In this chapter, we will explore the importance of finding inspiration in our lives and how we can use it to fuel our enthusiasm.

The Importance of Finding Inspiration:

Inspiration is a vital component of enthusiasm. Without inspiration, we can easily lose our motivation and drive to pursue our goals. When we are inspired, we feel energized, optimistic, and focused on what we want to achieve. Inspiration provides us with a sense of purpose and direction, helping us to overcome obstacles and persevere in the face of adversity.

However, finding inspiration can be challenging, especially

when we feel stuck, unmotivated, or overwhelmed. We may struggle to identify our passions or find meaning in our daily lives. It's important to remember that inspiration can come from many sources, and it doesn't have to be grand or earth-shattering. Sometimes, it's the small moments of beauty, kindness, or connection that can inspire us the most.

Ways to Find Inspiration:

– Connect with Nature: Spending time in nature can be a powerful source of inspiration. Whether it's taking a hike, going for a walk, or simply sitting outside, being in nature can help us feel connected to something greater than ourselves. The beauty and complexity of the natural world can inspire us to explore, create, and appreciate the world around us.

– Read and Learn: Reading books, articles, and other materials can expose us to new ideas, perspectives, and experiences. By learning about the world, we can expand our knowledge and understanding, and find inspiration in the stories of others. Reading can also help us to reflect on our own experiences and discover new insights and possibilities.

– Surround Yourself with Positive People: The people we surround ourselves with can have a significant impact on our inspiration levels. Being around positive, enthusiastic, and supportive individuals can lift our spirits, encourage us to pursue our goals, and help us stay motivated. Conversely, negative or unsupportive people can drain our energy and enthusiasm, making it harder to find inspiration.

– Pursue Your Passions: Engaging in activities that we love can be a great source of inspiration. When we are doing something that we are passionate about, we feel energized, fulfilled, and motivated. Whether it's a hobby, a creative pursuit, or a career, pursuing our passions can help us tap into our inner spark and find inspiration in our daily lives.

– Travel: Traveling can be an excellent way to find inspiration. By exploring new places, cultures, and experiences, we can broaden our horizons and discover new perspectives and ideas. Traveling can also help us to step out of our comfort zones and challenge ourselves, which can be a great source of inspiration and growth.

13: FINDING INSPIRATION TO FUEL YOUR ENTHUSI-ASM

Conclusion:

Finding inspiration is essential for cultivating enthusiasm in our lives. By connecting with nature, reading and learning, surrounding ourselves with positive people, pursuing our passions, and traveling, we can tap into our inner spark and find inspiration in our daily lives. Remember that inspiration can come from many sources, and it's important to be open to new experiences and possibilities. With a little effort and intention, we can find the inspiration we need to fuel our enthusiasm and achieve our goals.

14: The Power of Positive Thinking for Enthusiasm

Positive thinking is a powerful tool for cultivating enthusiasm in our lives. It is the act of deliberately focusing on positive thoughts and emotions, instead of dwelling on negative ones. Positive thinking can help us to feel more confident, motivated, and empowered to take action towards our goals. In this chapter, we will explore the ways in which positive thinking can fuel enthusiasm, and how to incorporate this practice into our daily lives.

Positive thinking begins with a mindset shift. It involves recognizing that our thoughts and beliefs can shape our reality, and that we have the power to choose which thoughts we give our attention to. When we focus on positive thoughts and feelings, we create a positive energy within ourselves that can attract positive outcomes and experiences into our lives. Conversely, when we dwell on negative thoughts, we can attract more negative experiences and feelings of pessimism.

One of the most effective ways to practice positive thinking is through affirmations. Affirmations are positive statements that we repeat to ourselves, which can help to repro-

gram our subconscious mind and shift our thoughts and beliefs towards the positive. Affirmations can be tailored to
any area of our lives that we want to focus on, such as our
career, relationships, or personal growth.

For example, if we are feeling discouraged about our career,
we might repeat an affirmation such as "I am capable and
competent in my work, and I attract success and abundance
into my life." If we are struggling with self-doubt, we might
repeat an affirmation such as "I am worthy and deserving of
love, success, and happiness." By repeating these affirmations regularly, we can begin to internalize these positive
beliefs and shift our mindset towards one of positivity and
confidence.

Another way to practice positive thinking is by focusing on
gratitude. Gratitude is the act of acknowledging and appre-
ciating the good things in our lives, no matter how small
they may seem. When we focus on gratitude, we shift our attention towards the positive aspects of our lives, which can
help to boost our mood and energy levels. This, in turn, can
fuel our enthusiasm and motivation to pursue our goals and
dreams.

14: THE POWER OF POSITIVE THINKING FOR ENTHU-SIASM

One simple way to practice gratitude is by keeping a gratitude journal. Each day, write down three things that you are grateful for, no matter how small they may seem. This could be anything from a delicious cup of coffee in the morning to a supportive friend or a new opportunity at work. By focusing on the positive aspects of our lives in this way, we can shift our mindset towards one of positivity and appreciation, which can help to fuel our enthusiasm for life.

In addition to affirmations and gratitude, there are many other ways to practice positive thinking in our daily lives. One effective method is to surround ourselves with positivity, whether that means spending time with uplifting people, listening to inspiring music or podcasts, or reading motivational books or articles. By exposing ourselves to positive messages and ideas, we can reinforce our positive beliefs and attitudes and stay motivated and enthusiastic.

Another way to cultivate positivity is through visualization. Visualization involves imagining ourselves achieving our goals and dreams in vivid detail. By picturing ourselves in a positive outcome, we can reinforce our belief in our ability to achieve that outcome, which can fuel our enthusiasm and

14: THE POWER OF POSITIVE THINKING FOR ENTHUSIASM

motivation to take action towards our goals.

Ultimately, positive thinking is a powerful tool for cultivating enthusiasm and achieving lasting success in every area of our lives. By shifting our mindset towards positivity and focusing on the good things in our lives, we can create a positive energy within ourselves that can attract more positive outcomes and experiences into our lives. With practice and persistence, we can learn to harness the power of positive thinking to unleash our inner spark and create a life we truly love.

15: The Importance of Setting Goals for Enthusiasm

Setting goals is an important aspect of achieving enthusiasm in your life. Goals give you something to work towards and provide a sense of direction, purpose, and motivation. Without goals, it's easy to become complacent and feel stagnant, leading to a lack of enthusiasm and drive.

There are many benefits to setting goals for enthusiasm, including:

— Clarity: When you set goals, you gain clarity on what you want to achieve. This clarity helps you focus your energy and efforts on the things that matter most to you.

— Motivation: Goals provide motivation to take action towards what you want to achieve. When you have a clear goal in mind, you're more likely to take the necessary steps to achieve it.

— Sense of accomplishment: When you set and achieve goals, you gain a sense of accomplishment that can boost your enthusiasm and confidence.

— Progress: Goals help you track your progress and celebrate your successes along the way, which can further fuel your enthusiasm.

To set effective goals for enthusiasm, it's important to follow the SMART goal-setting framework:

– Specific: Make your goals specific and clearly defined. For example, instead of setting a goal to "exercise more," set a goal to "exercise for 30 minutes, three times a week."

– Measurable: Make sure your goals are measurable so you can track your progress. This means setting goals that are quantifiable, such as "save $5,000 by the end of the year."

– Achievable: Set goals that are realistic and achievable based on your current circumstances and resources. Setting unattainable goals can lead to discouragement and a loss of enthusiasm.

– Relevant: Make sure your goals align with your overall values, interests, and priorities. Setting goals that are not relevant to your life can lead to a lack of motivation and enthusiasm.

– Time-bound: Set a specific timeline for achieving your

goals. This will help you stay focused and motivated, and provide a sense of urgency to take action.

When setting goals, it's important to think about both short-term and long-term goals. Short-term goals can provide a sense of immediate accomplishment and motivation, while long-term goals provide a sense of direction and purpose for the future.

It's also important to remember that goals can change and evolve over time. As you grow and change, your goals may shift, and that's okay. The important thing is to continue setting goals that align with your values, interests, and priorities.

In addition to setting goals, it's important to create a plan of action to achieve them. This includes breaking down your goals into smaller, manageable steps and creating a timeline for when you will complete each step. By having a clear plan of action, you can stay focused and motivated towards achieving your goals.

Finally, it's important to celebrate your successes along the way. This can include acknowledging your progress, rewarding yourself for achieving milestones, and reflecting on what you've learned throughout the process. Celebrating your successes can help boost your enthusiasm and motivation, and provide a sense of pride and accomplishment in what you've achieved.

In summary, setting goals is an important aspect of achieving enthusiasm in your life. By following the SMART goal-setting framework, creating a plan of action, and celebrating your successes along the way, you can cultivate a sense of direction, motivation, and purpose that can fuel your enthusiasm and lead to lasting success in every area of your being.

16: Overcoming Self-Doubt to Ignite Enthusiasm

Introduction

Self-doubt is a common obstacle that many people face on their journey towards enthusiasm and success. It can be a major roadblock that prevents you from achieving your goals and pursuing your passions. However, there are ways to overcome self-doubt and ignite enthusiasm in your life. In this chapter, we will explore the causes of self-doubt, its impact on your life, and effective strategies to overcome it and unlock your inner spark.

The Causes of Self-Doubt

Self-doubt can stem from a variety of factors, including past experiences, negative self-talk, fear of failure, and the opinions of others. Perhaps you've failed at a previous endeavor, leading to feelings of inadequacy and doubt in your abilities. Maybe you compare yourself to others and feel like you don't measure up. Or, it could be that you simply haven't been exposed to enough positive reinforcement and encouragement in your life.

16: OVERCOMING SELF-DOUBT TO IGNITE ENTHUSI-ASM

The Impact of Self-Doubt

Self-doubt can have a significant impact on your life, affecting your confidence, motivation, and overall well-being. It can prevent you from pursuing your passions and taking risks, leading to missed opportunities and unfulfilled potential. Self-doubt can also contribute to feelings of anxiety, depression, and low self-esteem, negatively impacting your mental and emotional health.

Strategies for Overcoming Self-Doubt and Igniting Enthusiasm

— Identify the source of your self-doubt. Understanding the root cause of your doubts and fears is the first step in overcoming them. Ask yourself what triggers your self-doubt, and reflect on past experiences that may have contributed to these feelings.

— Challenge negative self-talk. Replace negative thoughts with positive affirmations, such as "I am capable of achieving my goals" or "I am worthy of success". Focus on your strengths and accomplishments, rather than dwelling on past failures or perceived shortcomings.

– Set achievable goals. Break down your goals into smaller, manageable tasks, and celebrate each milestone as you achieve it. This will help you build momentum and increase your confidence as you move towards your larger objectives.

– Practice self-care. Take care of your physical, emotional, and mental health by getting enough sleep, exercising regularly, and engaging in activities that bring you joy and relaxation. This will help you build resilience and increase your ability to cope with stress and setbacks.

– Surround yourself with positive influences. Seek out supportive friends, family members, and mentors who can offer encouragement and feedback. Join a community or group of individuals who share your passions and interests, and who can provide a sense of camaraderie and shared purpose.

– Embrace failure as a learning opportunity. Accept that failure is a natural part of the journey towards success, and view it as an opportunity to learn and grow. Use setbacks as a chance to reflect on what went wrong and how you can improve in the future.

Conclusion

16: OVERCOMING SELF-DOUBT TO IGNITE ENTHUSI-ASM

Self-doubt can be a major obstacle to enthusiasm and success, but it is not insurmountable. By understanding the causes of self-doubt, challenging negative self-talk, setting achievable goals, practicing self-care, surrounding yourself with positive influences, and embracing failure as a learning opportunity, you can overcome your doubts and unlock your inner spark of enthusiasm. Remember, enthusiasm is not just a state of mind – it's a way of life that can transform every area of your being.

17: The Role of Self-Care in Fostering Enthusiasm

Introduction

Self-care is often overlooked in our busy lives. We are so focused on achieving our goals, taking care of others, and meeting deadlines that we forget to take care of ourselves. However, self-care is crucial to our well-being, and it plays a vital role in fostering enthusiasm. In this chapter, we will discuss the importance of self-care in fostering enthusiasm and provide some practical tips for incorporating self-care into your daily routine.

The Importance of Self-Care

Self-care is the practice of taking care of your physical, mental, and emotional health. It involves taking time for yourself, getting enough sleep, eating a healthy diet, exercising regularly, and engaging in activities that bring you joy and fulfillment. Self-care is essential for fostering enthusiasm because it allows you to recharge and replenish your energy. When you take care of yourself, you have more energy to pursue your passions, overcome challenges, and achieve your goals.

17: THE ROLE OF SELF-CARE IN FOSTERING ENTHUSI-ASM

Practical Tips for Incorporating Self-Care into Your Daily Routine

Here are some practical tips for incorporating self-care into your daily routine:

– Make Time for Yourself

Make sure to set aside time for yourself each day. This can be as simple as taking a 15-minute walk outside, reading a book, or meditating. Find an activity that you enjoy and make it a priority to do it every day.

– Get Enough Sleep

Getting enough sleep is essential for your physical and mental health. Aim to get 7-9 hours of sleep each night and establish a consistent sleep routine. This will help you feel more energized and focused during the day.

– Eat a Healthy Diet

Eating a healthy diet is essential for your overall well-being. Make sure to eat a variety of fruits, vegetables, whole grains, and lean protein. Avoid processed foods, sugary drinks, and excessive amounts of caffeine.

– Exercise Regularly

Regular exercise is important for maintaining your physical
and mental health. Find an activity that you enjoy and make
it a regular part of your routine. This could be anything
from going for a run, practicing yoga, or taking a dance
class.

– Practice Mindfulness

Mindfulness is the practice of being present in the moment
and focusing on your thoughts and feelings without judgment. This can help you reduce stress and increase your
overall sense of well-being. Try practicing mindfulness
through meditation or mindful breathing exercises.

– Engage in Activities That Bring You Joy

Engaging in activities that bring you joy is an important
part of self-care. This could be anything from painting, playing an instrument, or spending time with loved ones. Find
activities that bring you joy and make time for them regularly.

17: THE ROLE OF SELF-CARE IN FOSTERING ENTHUSI-ASM

Conclusion

Self-care is essential for fostering enthusiasm. By taking care of yourself, you can recharge your energy and cultivate a positive mindset that will help you pursue your passions and achieve your goals. Remember to make time for yourself, get enough sleep, eat a healthy diet, exercise regularly, practice mindfulness, and engage in activities that bring you joy. By incorporating these practices into your daily routine, you can unleash your inner spark and live a life filled with enthusiasm.

18: Using Visualization to Boost Enthusiasm

Visualization is a powerful tool that can help you to ignite your enthusiasm and reach your goals. By using your imagination to create vivid mental images of your desired outcome, you can harness the power of your mind to achieve your dreams. Visualization can help you to build confidence, increase focus, and enhance motivation. In this chapter, we'll explore the science behind visualization and provide tips for how to use this technique to boost your enthusiasm.

What is Visualization?

Visualization, also known as mental imagery or mental rehearsal, is the process of creating a vivid mental image of a desired outcome. It involves using your imagination to simulate the experience of achieving your goals in your mind. When you visualize, you engage your senses, including sight, sound, touch, smell, and taste, to create a sensory-rich experience in your mind. Visualization is not just about imagining what you want to achieve; it's about feeling as though you have already achieved it.

18: USING VISUALIZATION TO BOOST ENTHUSIASM

The Science Behind Visualization

The power of visualization lies in its ability to activate the same neural pathways in your brain that are activated when you actually perform the actions associated with your desired outcome. When you visualize an action, your brain processes the information in the same way it would if you were actually performing the action. Studies have shown that visualization can improve performance in a range of activities, including sports, music, and public speaking.

Visualization can also help to reduce anxiety and stress. When you visualize a positive outcome, your brain releases neurotransmitters, such as dopamine and serotonin, which can help to reduce stress and boost your mood. Visualization has even been shown to have a positive impact on physical health. Studies have found that visualization can help to lower blood pressure, reduce pain, and boost the immune system.

Tips for Using Visualization to Boost Enthusiasm

– Get into a relaxed state: Before you begin visualization, it's important to get into a relaxed state. You can do this by practicing deep breathing, progressive muscle relaxation, or meditation. When you're relaxed, your mind is more receptive to positive imagery.

– Choose a specific goal: Choose a specific goal that you want to achieve and focus your visualization on that goal. Make sure that your goal is realistic and achievable.

– Use vivid imagery: As you visualize, use all of your senses to create a vivid mental image of your desired outcome. Imagine yourself in the situation, using all of your senses to create a sensory-rich experience in your mind.

– Visualize yourself succeeding: When you visualize, always imagine yourself succeeding. Don't focus on potential obstacles or challenges; instead, focus on the positive outcome that you want to achieve.

– Practice regularly: Visualization is a skill that can be developed with practice. Set aside time each day to visualize your desired outcome. The more you practice, the easier it will become.

– Use affirmations: Affirmations are positive statements that can help to reinforce your visualization. Repeat positive affirmations to yourself, such as "I am confident and successful," as you visualize.

– Stay motivated: Visualization can help to boost your motivation, but it's important to stay motivated even when things get tough. Use your visualization practice to stay focused on your goals and remind yourself of why you started in the first place.

Conclusion

Visualization is a powerful tool that can help you to boost your enthusiasm and achieve your goals. By creating a vivid mental image of your desired outcome, you can activate the same neural pathways in your brain that are associated with actual performance. Visualization can help to reduce anxiety and stress, boost motivation, and improve overall wellbeing. By following the tips outlined in this chapter, you can use visualization to unlock your inner spark and achieve lasting success in every area of your life.

19: The Art of Letting Go to Make Room for Enthusiasm

Enthusiasm is a powerful force that can help you achieve great things in life, but sometimes it can be hard to find it when you're weighed down by past experiences, regrets, and negative emotions. This is where the art of letting go comes in.

Letting go is the process of releasing attachment to things that no longer serve us, whether it's a relationship, a job, a habit, or a belief. It's about acknowledging that holding on to the past can prevent us from moving forward and experiencing the joys of the present moment.

In order to cultivate enthusiasm, it's important to make room for it in your life. This means letting go of anything that is holding you back or causing negative emotions. Here are some tips for practicing the art of letting go:

– Identify what you need to let go of: Take some time to reflect on what is causing you stress, anxiety, or negativity in your life. It could be a job that no longer fulfills you, a toxic relationship, or a negative belief that is limiting your potential. Once you've identified what you need to let go of, you can begin the process of releasing it.

– Accept what you can't change: Sometimes we hold on to things that we have no control over, like the past or other people's actions. It's important to accept that we can't change the past and that we can't control other people's behavior. Instead, focus on what you can control, like your own thoughts and actions.

– Practice forgiveness: Holding on to anger, resentment, or grudges can weigh us down and prevent us from experiencing enthusiasm. Forgiveness is not about excusing bad behavior, but rather it's about releasing the negative emotions associated with it. When you forgive someone, you are freeing yourself from the burden of anger and resentment.

– Create a positive mindset: Letting go of negative thoughts and beliefs can be difficult, but it's essential for cultivating enthusiasm. Focus on the positive aspects of your life and practice gratitude for what you have. Surround yourself with positive people and affirmations that reinforce your positive mindset.

– Take action: Letting go of something doesn't mean giving

up or doing nothing. It means taking action to create the life you want. This might mean finding a new job, ending a toxic relationship, or adopting a healthier lifestyle. Taking action towards your goals will help you build momentum and create enthusiasm for your future.

The art of letting go is not easy, but it's essential for creating space in your life for enthusiasm to grow. By identifying what you need to let go of, accepting what you can't change, practicing forgiveness, creating a positive mindset, and taking action towards your goals, you can release the past and embrace the present with enthusiasm and joy.

20: The Benefits of Exercise for Enthusiasm

Introduction

When it comes to fostering enthusiasm in our lives, exercise can play a significant role. Not only does it benefit our physical health, but it also has a positive impact on our mental and emotional well-being. In this chapter, we will explore the many benefits of exercise for enthusiasm and how it can help us lead a more fulfilling and vibrant life.

Physical Benefits of Exercise

Exercise has numerous physical benefits that can help boost our enthusiasm. Regular exercise can help improve our cardiovascular health, strengthen our bones and muscles, and boost our energy levels. When we feel physically strong and healthy, we are more likely to approach life with enthusiasm and vitality.

Exercise also releases endorphins, the body's feel-good hormones, which can help reduce stress and anxiety. This can have a positive impact on our mood and overall sense of well-being, allowing us to approach life with more enthusiasm and optimism.

Mental Benefits of Exercise

In addition to its physical benefits, exercise also has numerous mental benefits. Regular exercise has been shown to improve our cognitive function, including our ability to think creatively and problem-solve. This can help us approach challenges in our lives with more enthusiasm and confidence.

Exercise can also help reduce symptoms of depression and anxiety, which can have a significant impact on our overall sense of well-being. When we feel mentally and emotionally balanced, we are more likely to approach life with enthusiasm and positivity.

Social Benefits of Exercise

Exercise can also have social benefits, which can help foster enthusiasm in our lives. Joining a fitness class or sports team can help us connect with others who share similar interests and goals. This sense of community and social support can be incredibly motivating and energizing, helping us approach life with more enthusiasm and purpose.

Furthermore, exercising with others can provide us with accountability and motivation. When we exercise with others, we are more likely to stick to our routine and push ourselves harder than we might on our own. This can help us achieve our fitness goals and approach life with more enthusiasm and determination.

Finding the Right Type of Exercise

When it comes to exercise, finding the right type for you is key to fostering enthusiasm. Some people thrive on high-intensity workouts, while others prefer gentler forms of exercise like yoga or walking. It's important to find an exercise routine that you enjoy and that feels sustainable for you.

Mixing up your exercise routine can also help keep things fresh and exciting. Trying new activities or joining a new fitness class can help keep you motivated and engaged. This can help foster enthusiasm for exercise and for life in general.

Incorporating Exercise into Your Daily Routine

Incorporating exercise into your daily routine can be challenging, but it's worth it for the many benefits it provides.

Finding ways to make exercise a habit, such as scheduling it into your calendar or finding a workout buddy, can help make it a regular part of your routine.

It's also important to be realistic about your exercise goals. Setting overly ambitious goals can lead to burnout or frustration, which can undermine your enthusiasm. Instead, set realistic goals and celebrate small victories along the way.

Conclusion

Exercise has numerous benefits for our physical, mental, and emotional well-being, all of which can help boost our enthusiasm for life. Incorporating exercise into our daily routine and finding the right type of exercise for us can help us lead a more vibrant, fulfilling life. By taking care of our physical health and mental well-being through exercise, we can approach life with enthusiasm and positivity.

21: How to Build Resilience for Enthusiasm

Resilience is an essential trait for anyone looking to cultivate enthusiasm and achieve lasting success in every area of their being. Life is full of ups and downs, and it's how we respond to adversity that determines our ability to bounce back and keep moving forward.

Fortunately, resilience is not something you're born with or without. It's a skill that can be developed with practice and determination. In this chapter, we'll explore the importance of resilience for cultivating enthusiasm, and provide you with practical strategies to help you build this critical skill.

Why Resilience is Important for Enthusiasm

Resilience is defined as the ability to recover quickly from difficulties and adapt to changing circumstances. In the pursuit of enthusiasm, resilience is critical because it helps us overcome setbacks and challenges that may otherwise derail us.

When we encounter obstacles, it's easy to become discouraged and lose our passion for the things we love. Resilience allows us to stay the course, even in the face of adversity. It helps us maintain our momentum and focus on the positive, even when things seem bleak.

Moreover, resilience is essential for maintaining our physical and mental health. When we're resilient, we're better equipped to manage stress, maintain healthy relationships, and enjoy a more balanced and fulfilling life.

Building Resilience for Enthusiasm

Now that we've explored the importance of resilience for cultivating enthusiasm, let's take a look at some practical strategies you can use to build this critical skill:

– Cultivate a Growth Mindset

A growth mindset is the belief that our abilities and talents can be developed through hard work, determination, and persistence. This mindset is essential for building resilience because it helps us view setbacks as opportunities for growth and learning.

To cultivate a growth mindset, start by challenging negative self-talk and limiting beliefs. Instead, focus on your strengths and potential for growth, and take proactive steps to improve your skills and knowledge.

– Practice Self-Care

Self-care is essential for building resilience because it helps us manage stress and maintain our physical and mental health. To practice self-care, make time for activities that nourish your mind, body, and spirit, such as exercise, meditation, and hobbies you enjoy.

– Build a Support System

Having a strong support system is critical for building resilience. Make an effort to cultivate healthy relationships with people who uplift and inspire you, and who will be there to support you when times get tough.

– Set Realistic Goals

Setting realistic goals is essential for building resilience because it helps us stay motivated and focused on our priorities. When setting goals, be sure to break them down into smaller, manageable steps, and celebrate your progress along the way.

21: HOW TO BUILD RESILIENCE FOR ENTHUSIASM

– Learn from Failure

Failure is an inevitable part of life, but it doesn't have to define us. Instead of viewing failure as a personal shortcoming, try to see it as an opportunity for growth and learning. Take the time to reflect on what went wrong and identify ways you can improve in the future.

– Practice Mindfulness

Mindfulness is the practice of being present and fully engaged in the moment. It's an effective tool for building resilience because it helps us manage stress, regulate our emotions, and maintain a positive outlook.

To practice mindfulness, try incorporating daily meditation, deep breathing exercises, or other relaxation techniques into your routine.

Conclusion

Building resilience is critical for cultivating enthusiasm and achieving lasting success in every area of your being. By cultivating a growth mindset, practicing self-care, building a support system, setting realistic goals, learning from failure, and practicing mindfulness, you can develop the resilience you need to overcome setbacks and keep moving forward. With time and practice, you'll find that resilience becomes a natural part of who you are, helping you cultivate enthusiasm and achieve your goals with greater ease and confidence.

22: The Importance of a Support System for Enthusiasm

Enthusiasm can be contagious, but it can also be easily dampened by negative external factors or inner doubts. That's why having a strong support system is crucial for maintaining and fueling enthusiasm.

A support system can come in many forms: friends, family, mentors, colleagues, coaches, or even online communities. The key is to surround yourself with people who encourage, inspire, challenge, and believe in you. These are the people who lift you up when you're feeling down, cheer you on when you're making progress, and offer constructive feedback when you're stuck or making mistakes.

Here are some reasons why having a support system is important for fostering enthusiasm:

– Validation and encouragement: Enthusiasm can often feel like a vulnerable emotion because it exposes our hopes, dreams, and aspirations to the world. Having a supportive person or group can provide validation and encouragement, which reinforces the belief that what we're pursuing is worthy and meaningful. When someone tells us "You got this!" or "I believe in you!", it can give us the boost of confidence and energy we need to keep going.

– Accountability and motivation: Sometimes enthusiasm alone is not enough to sustain us through the ups and downs of a project or a goal. That's where accountability and motivation come in. When we share our enthusiasm and plans with others, we are more likely to follow through with them because we don't want to disappoint or let down those who are rooting for us. Moreover, seeing others' progress or success can motivate us to work harder and smarter.

– Feedback and perspective: Enthusiasm can also make us blind to our weaknesses or blind spots. That's why having someone who can offer honest feedback and perspective can be invaluable. They can point out areas where we need to improve or adjust our approach, as well as highlight our strengths and talents that we may overlook. Furthermore, they can offer a fresh perspective that we may not have considered, which can spark new ideas or insights.

– Emotional support: Enthusiasm can also be vulnerable because it exposes us to the risk of failure or disappointment. Having a supportive person or group can provide emotional support during tough times, such as setbacks, rejections, or self-doubt. They can offer empathy, understanding, and a safe space to express our fears or frustrations. Moreover, they can share their own stories of resilience and overcoming challenges, which can inspire and reassure us that we're not alone.

– Networking and opportunities: Finally, having a supportive network can also open up new doors and opportunities that we may not have access to otherwise. They can introduce us to new people, resources, or ideas that can expand our horizons and enrich our enthusiasm. Moreover, they can vouch for us or recommend us to potential employers, clients, or collaborators, which can boost our credibility and visibility.

In summary, a support system is a powerful tool for building and sustaining enthusiasm. By surrounding ourselves with positive, supportive, and helpful people, we can overcome obstacles, learn from feedback, stay accountable, and nurture our passion. However, building a support system takes time, effort, and vulnerability. It requires us to reach out, share our enthusiasm, and listen to others. It also requires us to be selective and discerning about who we let into our inner circle, as not everyone will share our values, goals, or vision. Nevertheless, the rewards of having a strong support system are worth the investment, as they can help us unleash our inner spark and achieve lasting success in every area of our being.

23: How to Use Affirmations to Boost Enthusiasm

Affirmations are powerful tools that can help you boost your enthusiasm and achieve your goals. When used correctly, they can help you transform your mindset, increase your self-confidence, and overcome any obstacles that come your way. In this chapter, we will explore the power of affirmations and provide you with practical tips for using them to ignite your inner spark and achieve lasting success in every area of your life.

What are Affirmations?

Affirmations are positive statements that you repeat to yourself on a regular basis. They are designed to help you reprogram your subconscious mind and replace negative thoughts and beliefs with positive ones. When you repeat affirmations to yourself, you create new neural pathways in your brain that support the positive changes you want to make in your life.

Affirmations are a simple yet effective way to boost your enthusiasm and achieve your goals. They work by shifting your focus from what you don't want to what you do want, and by helping you stay focused on your desired outcome.

How to Use Affirmations to Boost Enthusiasm

Here are some practical tips for using affirmations to boost your enthusiasm:

– Identify Your Desired Outcome

The first step in using affirmations is to identify your desired outcome. What do you want to achieve? What is your goal? Once you have identified your desired outcome, you can create an affirmation that reflects that outcome.

For example, if your goal is to become more confident, your affirmation might be: "I am confident and self-assured in everything I do."

– Create a Positive Affirmation

When creating your affirmation, it's important to make sure it is positive and in the present tense. This helps your brain believe that the affirmation is true, even if it hasn't happened yet.

For example, instead of saying "I will be confident," say "I am confident." This puts your brain in a positive state and helps you focus on the outcome you want to achieve.

– Repeat Your Affirmation Regularly

To get the most out of affirmations, it's important to repeat them regularly. This helps your brain create new neural pathways that support the positive changes you want to make in your life.

You can repeat your affirmation in the morning when you wake up, throughout the day, and before you go to bed at night. You can also write your affirmation down and place it somewhere where you will see it regularly, such as on your bathroom mirror or your computer screen.

– Visualize Your Desired Outcome

Visualization is a powerful tool that can help you manifest your desired outcome. When you visualize your desired outcome, you create a mental picture of what you want to achieve. This helps your brain believe that the outcome is possible and increases your enthusiasm for achieving it.

23: HOW TO USE AFFIRMATIONS TO BOOST ENTHUSI-ASM

To use visualization, close your eyes and imagine yourself achieving your desired outcome. Picture yourself feeling happy, confident, and fulfilled. See yourself taking action towards your goal and achieving success. The more vividly you can picture your desired outcome, the more effective your visualization will be.

– Use Affirmations to Overcome Obstacles

Affirmations can also be used to overcome obstacles and challenges that come your way. When you encounter an obstacle, it's easy to become discouraged and lose your enthusiasm for achieving your goal. However, affirmations can help you stay focused and motivated, even in the face of adversity.

For example, if you encounter an obstacle that makes you doubt your ability to achieve your goal, you can repeat an affirmation such as: "I am strong, capable, and resilient. I can overcome any obstacle that comes my way."

Conclusion

Affirmations are a powerful tool that can help you boost

your enthusiasm and achieve your goals. By identifying your desired outcome, creating a positive affirmation, repeating it regularly, visualizing your desired outcome and using affirmations to overcome obstacles, you can ignite your inner spark and transform your life.

Using affirmations can be a simple yet effective way to shift your mindset and overcome any negative thoughts or beliefs that may be holding you back. By focusing on the positive and repeating affirmations that reflect your desired outcome, you can reprogram your subconscious mind and create new neural pathways that support your goals and dreams.

Remember, enthusiasm is contagious, and when you are enthusiastic about your life and your goals, you can inspire others to be enthusiastic too. So go ahead, unleash your inner spark, and use affirmations to transform your life and achieve lasting success in every area of your being.

24: The Role of Creativity in Fostering Enthusiasm

Creativity is an essential component of enthusiasm, and it plays a significant role in fostering and sustaining enthusiasm in every area of your life. In this chapter, we will explore the importance of creativity in fostering enthusiasm and provide you with practical tips for using creativity to ignite your inner spark and achieve lasting success.

What is Creativity?

Creativity is the ability to think outside the box, to generate new ideas, and to solve problems in innovative ways. It is the ability to create something new and unique, to see the world in a different way, and to express yourself creatively through various mediums.

Creativity can take many forms, including art, music, writing, cooking, or even problem-solving in the workplace. It is a skill that can be developed and nurtured over time, and it can be an invaluable asset in every area of your life.

The Role of Creativity in Fostering Enthusiasm

Creativity plays a vital role in fostering enthusiasm in every area of your life. Here are some of the ways in which creativity can help ignite your inner spark and keep it burning brightly:

– Creativity Brings Joy and Passion

When you engage in creative activities, you experience joy and passion. You get lost in the process of creating, and you feel a sense of accomplishment when you finish your project. This joy and passion can help ignite your enthusiasm and keep it burning brightly.

– Creativity Inspires Innovation

Creativity inspires innovation and new ideas. When you think creatively, you can come up with new solutions to problems, new ways of doing things, and new products and services. This innovation can help you stay enthusiastic and excited about your work, your relationships, and your life.

– Creativity Fosters Personal Growth

Engaging in creative activities can foster personal growth and development. It can help you discover new talents and strengths, improve your self-esteem, and boost your confidence. This personal growth can help you stay enthusiastic and excited about your life and your goals.

– Creativity Fosters Resilience

Creativity can help you develop resilience and the ability to bounce back from setbacks and challenges. When you engage in creative activities, you learn to embrace mistakes and see them as opportunities for growth and learning. This resilience can help you stay enthusiastic and motivated, even in the face of adversity.

– Creativity Connects You to Others

Engaging in creative activities can also help you connect with others. It can help you form new friendships, find common interests, and build a sense of community. This connection can help you stay enthusiastic and excited about your relationships and your social life.

Practical Tips for Using Creativity to Foster Enthusiasm

Here are some practical tips for using creativity to foster enthusiasm in every area of your life:

24: THE ROLE OF CREATIVITY IN FOSTERING ENTHU-SIASM

– Try Something New

One of the best ways to ignite your creativity is to try something new. Sign up for a dance class, try a new recipe, or take up a new hobby. Trying something new can help you get out of your comfort zone and experience new things, which can help foster enthusiasm and creativity.

– Set Aside Time for Creative Activities

Make time for creative activities in your daily or weekly routine. Set aside a specific time each day or each week for writing, painting, playing music, or engaging in whatever creative activity you enjoy. This can help you stay committed to your creative pursuits and keep your enthusiasm burning brightly.

– Collaborate with Others

Collaborating with others can be a great way to foster creativity and enthusiasm. Join a writing group, a painting class, or a music ensemble. Collaborating with others can help you find new inspiration, learn new techniques, and build connections with others who share your passion.

24: THE ROLE OF CREATIVITY IN FOSTERING ENTHU-SIASM

– Embrace Your Mistakes

Don't be afraid to make mistakes when engaging in creative activities. Embracing your mistakes can help you see them as opportunities for growth and learning, rather than as failures. This can help you stay enthusiastic and motivated, even when things don't go as planned.

– Take Breaks and Relax

Taking breaks and relaxing is essential for fostering creativity and enthusiasm. When you take a break, you allow your mind to rest and recharge, which can help you come up with new ideas and approaches. Relaxation can also help you reduce stress and anxiety, which can help you stay focused and motivated.

– Keep an Open Mind

Keeping an open mind is crucial for fostering creativity and enthusiasm. Don't be afraid to try new things or to think outside the box. Be open to new ideas and approaches, and don't limit yourself to what you think you already know. Keeping an open mind can help you stay curious, motivated, and enthusiastic about your life and your goals.

Conclusion

In conclusion, creativity plays a vital role in fostering enthusiasm in every area of your life. By engaging in creative
activities, you can bring joy and passion into your life, inspire innovation and new ideas, foster personal growth and
resilience, connect with others, and stay enthusiastic and
motivated, even in the face of adversity.

Remember, creativity is a skill that can be developed and
nurtured over time. By trying something new, setting aside
time for creative activities, collaborating with others, embracing your mistakes, taking breaks and relaxing, and
keeping an open mind, you can ignite your inner spark and
achieve lasting success in every area of your being.

25: How to Use Failure to Fuel Enthusiasm

Introduction

Failure is a word that often strikes fear into the hearts of many. It can make you feel defeated, embarrassed, and even hopeless. However, failure can also be a powerful tool for fostering enthusiasm and success. In this chapter, we'll explore how to use failure to fuel enthusiasm and turn setbacks into opportunities for growth and transformation.

– Embrace Failure

The first step in using failure to fuel enthusiasm is to embrace it. Failure is a natural part of life, and everyone experiences it at some point. Instead of avoiding or denying failure, embrace it as an opportunity for growth and learning. By acknowledging your failures, you can begin to understand what went wrong, and what you can do differently in the future.

– Learn from Failure

Once you've embraced failure, the next step is to learn from it. Failure can be a valuable teacher, providing you with feedback and insights that can help you improve your performance and avoid making the same mistakes again. Analyze your failures and try to identify the specific areas where you need to improve. Use this information to develop a plan for moving forward and achieving your goals.

– Reframe Failure as Feedback

One way to use failure to fuel enthusiasm is to reframe it as feedback. Instead of seeing failure as a personal flaw or a reflection of your worth, see it as information that can help you improve. Reframing failure as feedback can help you stay motivated and focused on your goals, rather than getting bogged down by feelings of shame or self-doubt.

– Celebrate Your Efforts

Another way to use failure to fuel enthusiasm is to celebrate your efforts, even when they don't lead to immediate success. Acknowledge the hard work and dedication that went into your efforts, and take pride in the progress you've made. Celebrating your efforts can help you stay enthusiastic and motivated, even in the face of setbacks and challenges.

25: HOW TO USE FAILURE TO FUEL ENTHUSIASM

– Use Failure as Fuel

Perhaps the most powerful way to use failure to fuel enthusiasm is to use it as fuel. Instead of letting failure defeat you, use it as motivation to push yourself harder and strive for even greater success. Use your failures as a source of inspiration and determination, and let them fuel your enthusiasm and passion for achieving your goals.

– Maintain a Growth Mindset

Finally, to use failure to fuel enthusiasm, you need to maintain a growth mindset. A growth mindset is a belief that your abilities and skills can be developed through hard work, dedication, and persistence. When you have a growth mindset, you see failure as an opportunity for growth and learning, rather than a fixed state of ability. By maintaining a growth mindset, you can stay enthusiastic and motivated, even when facing challenges and setbacks.

Conclusion

In conclusion, failure can be a powerful tool for fueling enthusiasm and success. By embracing failure, learning from it, reframing it as feedback, celebrating your efforts, using it as fuel, and maintaining a growth mindset, you can turn setbacks into opportunities for growth and transformation. Remember, failure is not the end of the road, but rather a stepping stone on your journey to achieving your goals and creating a life you love.

26: The Power of Play for Enthusiasm

Introduction

When was the last time you played? Not just engaged in a hobby or activity, but truly played without any agenda or goal in mind? Play is often associated with childhood, but it is an essential component of a happy and fulfilling life at any age. In this chapter, we'll explore the power of play for fostering enthusiasm and enhancing every area of your being.

– What is Play?

Before we dive into the power of play, it's important to define what we mean by "play." Play can be defined as any activity that is engaged in purely for the sake of enjoyment, with no specific goal or outcome in mind. It can include anything from sports and games to creative pursuits like painting, dancing, or singing.

– Benefits of Play

Play is not just fun - it also has numerous physical, mental, and emotional benefits. Here are just a few of the ways play can enhance your life:

– Boosts creativity and problem-solving skills

– Improves cognitive function and memory

– Relieves stress and anxiety

– Increases social connection and communication skills

– Boosts physical fitness and overall health

– The Science of Play

Play isn't just a frivolous activity - it's actually hardwired into our brains. Studies have shown that play activates the same reward centers in the brain as food and sex, and can release feel-good hormones like dopamine and endorphins. Additionally, play has been linked to the growth and development of brain cells in key areas related to learning and memory.

– Incorporating Play into Your Life

Now that we've established the benefits and science of play, it's time to explore how to incorporate more play into your life. Here are a few strategies for infusing play into your routine:

– Make time for play: Schedule regular playtime into your schedule, just like you would any other important activity or appointment.

– Try new activities: Explore new hobbies or activities that you've always been interested in but never had the time or opportunity to try.

– Embrace creativity: Engage in creative pursuits like drawing, writing, or playing music, without worrying about the outcome or whether it's "good enough."

– Play with others: Engage in group activities like team sports or game nights to enhance social connection and communication skills.

– Make it a habit: Incorporate play into your daily routine, whether it's taking a few minutes to dance around your living room or playing a quick game of chess during your lunch break.

– The Power of Play for Enthusiasm

Finally, let's explore the power of play for fostering enthusiasm. Play can be a powerful source of inspiration, creativity, and motivation. When you engage in play, you tap into your natural sense of curiosity and wonder, and open yourself up to new possibilities and experiences. Additionally, play can provide a much-needed break from the stresses and responsibilities of daily life, allowing you to recharge and return to your tasks with renewed energy and enthusiasm.

Conclusion

In conclusion, play is not just for children - it's an essential component of a happy and fulfilling life at any age. By embracing play and incorporating it into your routine, you can reap the numerous physical, mental, and emotional benefits it has to offer, while also enhancing your enthusiasm and zest for life. Remember, play is not just a luxury - it's a necessity for a healthy, happy, and vibrant life. So go ahead, let yourself play, and see the transformative power it can have in every area of your being.

27: How to Stay Motivated in the Face of Challenges

Introduction

In life, we all face challenges and obstacles that can derail our enthusiasm and motivation. Whether it's a setback at work, a health issue, or a personal struggle, staying motivated and focused can be difficult when the going gets tough. In this chapter, we'll explore some strategies for staying motivated in the face of challenges, so you can continue to pursue your goals and dreams with enthusiasm and passion.

– Identify Your Why

When faced with challenges, it's easy to lose sight of why you started on your path in the first place. That's why it's important to take a step back and remind yourself of your why. Ask yourself: What inspired you to pursue your goal or dream? What motivates you to keep going even when the going gets tough? By identifying your why, you can reconnect with your purpose and reignite your passion.

– Break Your Goal Down into Manageable Steps

Sometimes, challenges can seem overwhelming, and it can

be difficult to know where to begin. That's why it's important to break your goal down into manageable steps. Start by identifying the smallest, most achievable action you can take towards your goal, and focus on that. Once you've accomplished that step, move on to the next one. This approach can help you stay motivated by giving you a sense of progress and accomplishment, even in the face of challenges.

– Focus on the Positives

When facing challenges, it's easy to get bogged down in negativity and pessimism. However, focusing on the positives can help you stay motivated and energized. Take time to reflect on your successes and accomplishments, no matter how small they may seem. Celebrate your progress and focus on what you've learned from your challenges. By maintaining a positive mindset, you can stay motivated and resilient.

– Find Support

Facing challenges alone can be isolating and demotivating. That's why it's important to find support from others who can offer encouragement and motivation. This support can come from family, friends, or even a mentor or coach who can offer guidance and perspective. Additionally, consider joining a support group or online community of like-minded individuals who can relate to your struggles and offer support.

– Take Care of Yourself

Finally, when facing challenges, it's important to take care of yourself. This means getting enough rest, eating well, and engaging in self-care activities that help you recharge and rejuvenate. When you're feeling stressed and overwhelmed, taking a break to do something you enjoy, like reading a book or going for a walk, can help you stay motivated and energized.

Conclusion

In conclusion, staying motivated in the face of challenges is an essential component of achieving lasting success and fulfillment. By identifying your why, breaking your goal down into manageable steps, focusing on the positives, finding support, and taking care of yourself, you can stay motivated and passionate, even in the face of adversity. Remember, challenges are a natural part of the journey towards success, but with the right mindset and strategies, you can overcome them and emerge stronger, more motivated, and more enthusiastic than ever before.

28: The Benefits of Taking Risks for Enthusiasm

Introduction

When it comes to achieving success and fulfillment in life, taking risks can be a powerful tool. By stepping outside your comfort zone and embracing the unknown, you can unlock new opportunities and experiences that can ignite your enthusiasm and passion. In this chapter, we'll explore the benefits of taking risks for enthusiasm, and provide some tips for how to do so effectively.

– Overcoming Fear and Building Resilience

One of the most significant benefits of taking risks is that it can help you overcome fear and build resilience. Fear is a natural human response to the unknown, and it can hold us back from pursuing our goals and dreams. However, by taking calculated risks and facing our fears, we can build resilience and develop the confidence to take on even greater challenges. This resilience can then translate into other areas of our lives, helping us become more confident and enthusiastic overall.

28: THE BENEFITS OF TAKING RISKS FOR ENTHUSI-ASM

– Unlocking New Opportunities

Another benefit of taking risks is that it can unlock new opportunities that we may not have otherwise encountered. When we step outside our comfort zone, we expose ourselves to new experiences, people, and perspectives that can broaden our horizons and help us grow. These new opportunities can also ignite our passion and enthusiasm by providing a sense of purpose and fulfillment.

– Learning and Growth

Taking risks can also help us learn and grow in ways that may not be possible through more conventional means. When we take risks, we must adapt and learn quickly to navigate new situations and challenges. This can help us develop new skills, knowledge, and perspectives that can enhance our personal and professional development.

– Overcoming Limiting Beliefs

Often, we hold ourselves back from taking risks because of limiting beliefs about our abilities or the world around us. However, taking risks can help us overcome these limiting beliefs by showing us what is possible when we stretch beyond our perceived limitations. By taking risks and pushing ourselves to new heights, we can break down these limiting beliefs and unleash our full potential.

– Achieving Lasting Success and Fulfillment

Ultimately, the benefits of taking risks for enthusiasm are in achieving lasting success and fulfillment. By taking risks, we can unlock new opportunities, overcome fear and limiting beliefs, and develop resilience and confidence that can help us achieve our goals and dreams. This success and fulfillment can then fuel our enthusiasm and passion, creating a virtuous cycle of growth and development.

Tips for Taking Risks Effectively

Taking risks can be daunting, but there are some tips you can follow to do so effectively:

– Define your goal and understand the potential risks and benefits.

– Start small and build up to bigger risks over time.

– Embrace failure as a natural part of the process and learn from it.

– Surround yourself with a supportive network of friends, family, and mentors who can provide guidance and encouragement.

– Take calculated risks and make informed decisions based on research and analysis.

Conclusion

In conclusion, taking risks can be a powerful tool for igniting enthusiasm and achieving lasting success and fulfillment. By overcoming fear and limiting beliefs, unlocking new opportunities, and building resilience and confidence, taking risks can help us grow and develop in ways that can transform our lives for the better. With the right mindset and approach, taking risks can be a thrilling and rewarding journey that can lead to a life of passion, purpose, and fulfillment.

29: The Importance of Authenticity for Enthusiasm

Introduction:

Authenticity is the foundation of enthusiasm. When we are true to ourselves, we are more likely to feel energized and engaged in what we are doing. Authenticity means being genuine and honest, both with ourselves and with others. It requires us to identify our values, beliefs, and passions, and to live in alignment with them. In this chapter, we will explore the importance of authenticity for enthusiasm and provide tips on how to cultivate it in your life.

What is Authenticity?

Authenticity is a state of being true to oneself. It involves being genuine and honest with ourselves and with others. It requires us to identify our values, beliefs, and passions and to live in alignment with them. Authenticity involves self-awareness and the ability to express our thoughts and emotions honestly and respectfully.

The Importance of Authenticity for Enthusiasm:

Authenticity is essential for enthusiasm because it allows us to connect with our inner selves and to live a life that is aligned with our values and passions. When we are authentic, we are more likely to feel energized and engaged in what we are doing. We are less likely to feel drained or burnt out because we are not pretending to be someone we are not.

Being authentic also enables us to connect with others on a deeper level. When we are genuine and honest, we create trust and build stronger relationships. Authenticity allows us to be vulnerable and to show our true selves to others, which can lead to more meaningful connections.

Tips for Cultivating Authenticity:

– Identify your values and passions: To be authentic, you must first identify your values and passions. What is important to you? What motivates and inspires you? Take the time to reflect on these questions and identify the things that make you feel most alive.

– Be honest with yourself: Authenticity requires self-awareness and honesty. Take the time to reflect on your thoughts, feelings, and beliefs. Be honest with yourself about your strengths and weaknesses, and about the things that make you happy and unhappy.

– Express yourself honestly: To be authentic, you must be able to express your thoughts and emotions honestly and respectfully. Speak your truth, even if it is difficult, but do so in a way that is respectful of others.

– Don't compare yourself to others: Authenticity means being true to yourself, not trying to be like someone else. Avoid comparing yourself to others and focus on living your own life in alignment with your values and passions.

– Embrace your uniqueness: Being authentic means embracing your uniqueness. Celebrate your quirks and idiosyncrasies, and don't be afraid to show your true self to others.

Conclusion:

Authenticity is essential for enthusiasm because it allows us to connect with our inner selves and to live a life that is aligned with our values and passions. It enables us to connect with others on a deeper level and to build stronger relationships. To cultivate authenticity, identify your values and passions, be honest with yourself, express yourself honestly, avoid comparing yourself to others, and embrace your uniqueness. By living authentically, you can unleash your inner spark and create a life you love.

30: How to Create a Plan for Enthusiasm

Enthusiasm is a powerful force that can transform your life and help you achieve success in every area of your being. However, harnessing this energy requires more than just positive thinking and wishful dreaming. To truly unleash your inner spark, you need a solid plan that will guide you through the ups and downs of your journey.

Creating a plan for enthusiasm involves four essential steps: defining your goals, identifying your obstacles, developing a strategy, and taking action.

Step One: Define Your Goals

Before you can create a plan for enthusiasm, you need to know what you want to achieve. Start by setting specific, measurable, and realistic goals for yourself. Ask yourself questions like:

– What do I want to accomplish in my personal life?

– What do I want to achieve in my career?

– What kind of relationships do I want to have?

– What kind of person do I want to become?

Be as specific as possible when defining your goals. Don't just say, "I want to be happy," or "I want to make more money." Instead, break down your goals into actionable steps that you can take to make them a reality.

For example, if your goal is to improve your physical health, your action steps might include:

– Going to the gym three times a week

– Eating a balanced diet with plenty of fruits and vegetables

– Drinking at least eight glasses of water a day

– Getting enough sleep each night

– Meditating or practicing yoga to reduce stress

Step Two: Identify Your Obstacles

Once you have a clear idea of what you want to achieve, it's time to identify the obstacles that stand in your way. These obstacles might be external, such as a lack of time or re-sources, or internal, such as fear, self-doubt, or negative self-talk.

Take some time to reflect on the obstacles that have held you back in the past. Ask yourself:

– What are my biggest fears?

– What negative thoughts or beliefs do I have about myself?

– What external factors have prevented me from achieving my goals in the past?

– How have I dealt with setbacks or failures in the past?

By identifying your obstacles, you can develop strategies to overcome them and stay on track towards your goals.

Step Three: Develop a Strategy

Once you know your goals and obstacles, it's time to develop a strategy for achieving your goals. This strategy should include specific action steps that you can take to overcome your obstacles and make progress towards your goals.

Here are some tips for developing a successful strategy:

– Break down your goals into smaller, manageable tasks that you can accomplish in a day or a week.

– Create a timeline for each task to keep yourself accountable and on track.

– Identify the resources and support that you need to achieve your goals, such as a mentor, a coach, or a supportive community.

– Develop a plan for dealing with setbacks and obstacles when they arise.

– Celebrate your successes along the way to stay motivated and inspired.

Step Four: Take Action

The final step in creating a plan for enthusiasm is to take action. It's not enough to just have a plan - you need to put it into action and make it a reality.

Here are some tips for taking action:

– Start small and build momentum over time.

– Stay focused on your goals and remind yourself why they are important to you.

– Use positive self-talk to overcome negative thoughts and beliefs.

– Stay flexible and adapt your plan as needed.

– Celebrate your progress and keep moving forward.

In conclusion, creating a plan for enthusiasm is essential if you want to unleash your inner spark and achieve lasting success in every area of your being. By defining your goals, identifying your obstacles, developing a strategy, and taking action, you can transform your life and create a future that inspires you. Remember that enthusiasm is a journey, not a destination. It requires consistent effort and a willingness to learn and grow.

As you work towards your goals, be kind to yourself and remember that setbacks and failures are a natural part of the process. Don't let them discourage you or make you give up. Instead, use them as opportunities to learn, grow, and improve.

It's also important to surround yourself with positive and supportive people who will encourage and uplift you on your journey. Seek out mentors, coaches, or a community of like-minded individuals who share your goals and can provide you with the support and guidance you need to succeed.

Finally, don't forget to have fun and enjoy the process. Enthusiasm is contagious, and when you approach your goals with a positive and joyful attitude, you'll attract more opportunities and success into your life.

In summary, creating a plan for enthusiasm is a crucial step towards unlocking your full potential and achieving lasting success. By defining your goals, identifying your obstacles, developing a strategy, and taking action, you can unleash your inner spark and create a life you love. Remember to stay focused, stay positive, and enjoy the journey!

31: The Role of Accountability in Fostering Enthusiasm

Accountability is a crucial component of fostering enthusiasm and achieving lasting success in every area of your being. It involves taking responsibility for your actions, holding yourself accountable for your goals, and staying on track towards your desired outcomes.

In this chapter, we'll explore the role of accountability in fostering enthusiasm and how you can use it to unlock your full potential and achieve your goals.

The Benefits of Accountability

Accountability has numerous benefits when it comes to fostering enthusiasm and achieving success. Here are just a few:

– It helps you stay focused on your goals. When you have someone or something holding you accountable, you're more likely to stay on track towards your desired outcomes. This can help you stay focused and motivated even when you face challenges or setbacks.

– It provides you with support and guidance. Having an accountability partner, coach, or mentor can provide you with the support and guidance you need to succeed. They can offer valuable feedback, advice, and encouragement along the way.

– It helps you overcome self-doubt and negative self-talk. When you're held accountable, you're forced to confront your self-doubt and negative self-talk. This can help you develop a more positive mindset and belief in your ability to achieve your goals.

– It promotes personal growth and development. Accountability challenges you to step outside of your comfort zone and take risks. This can help you grow and develop as a person and achieve things you never thought possible.

Types of Accountability

There are several types of accountability that you can use to foster enthusiasm and achieve your goals. Here are a few:

– Self-Accountability: This type of accountability involves holding yourself responsible for your actions and outcomes. It requires discipline, self-awareness, and a willingness to take ownership of your mistakes and shortcomings.

– Accountability Partner: An accountability partner is someone who holds you responsible for your actions and outcomes. This could be a friend, family member, or colleague who shares your goals and is committed to helping you achieve them.

– Coach or Mentor: A coach or mentor is a professional who provides you with guidance, feedback, and support as you work towards your goals. They can help you identify your strengths and weaknesses, develop a plan for success, and hold you accountable for your progress.

– Online Communities: Online communities can provide you with a sense of accountability and support as you work towards your goals. They can offer a space to connect with like-minded individuals, share your progress, and receive feedback and encouragement.

How to Foster Accountability

Fostering accountability requires a conscious effort to take ownership of your goals and outcomes. Here are a few tips to help you foster accountability in your life:

– Set Clear Goals: Setting clear, specific, and measurable goals is essential for accountability. It provides you with a clear target to aim for and makes it easier to track your progress.

– Find an Accountability Partner: Find someone who shares your goals and is committed to helping you achieve them. This could be a friend, family member, or colleague. Make sure to communicate your goals clearly and establish a plan for accountability.

– Hire a Coach or Mentor: A coach or mentor can provide you with professional guidance, feedback, and support. They can help you identify your strengths and weaknesses, develop a plan for success, and hold you accountable for your progress.

– Join Online Communities: Join online communities that align with your goals and interests. These communities can provide you with a sense of accountability and support as you work towards your goals.

31: THE ROLE OF ACCOUNTABILITY IN FOSTERING ENTHUSIASM

– Use Technology: Use technology to help you stay accountable. Apps and tools like habit trackers, goal-setting apps, and accountability groups can help you stay on track towards your desired outcomes.

In conclusion, accountability is a crucial component of fostering enthusiasm and achieving success in every area of your life. By taking ownership of your goals, finding an accountability partner, hiring a coach or mentor, joining online communities, and using technology, you can stay on track towards your desired outcomes and unlock your full potential.

Remember, accountability is not about punishment or blame. It's about taking responsibility for your actions and outcomes, and using that responsibility to create positive change in your life. When you're held accountable, you're more likely to stay focused, motivated, and on track towards your goals.

However, it's important to remember that accountability is not a one-size-fits-all solution. Different people respond to different forms of accountability. Some people thrive with a supportive accountability partner, while others prefer the guidance of a professional coach or mentor. Experiment with different forms of accountability until you find what works best for you.

In addition to fostering accountability, it's also important to celebrate your successes along the way. Recognize your progress and accomplishments, and use them as motivation to keep pushing forward towards your goals. Remember, enthusiasm is a journey, not a destination. Enjoy the process and celebrate every step of the way.

In summary, accountability plays a crucial role in fostering enthusiasm and achieving lasting success in every area of your being. By taking ownership of your goals, finding an accountability partner, hiring a coach or mentor, joining online communities, and using technology, you can stay on track towards your desired outcomes and unlock your full potential. Remember to celebrate your successes and enjoy the journey towards achieving your goals.

32: The Importance of Balance for Enthusiasm

In today's fast-paced and demanding world, it's easy to get caught up in the daily grind and forget about the importance of balance in our lives. We often prioritize work and other obligations over our personal lives, leading to burnout, stress, and a lack of enthusiasm for the things we used to love.

The truth is, balance is crucial for fostering enthusiasm and achieving lasting success in every area of your being. When your life is balanced, you have more energy, focus, and creativity to pursue your passions, overcome obstacles, and create a life you love.

So how do you create balance in your life? It starts by identifying your priorities and setting boundaries. Determine what's most important to you and make those things a priority. This could include your health, relationships, career, hobbies, or personal growth.

Next, set boundaries to protect your time and energy. Learn to say no to things that don't align with your priorities, and delegate tasks or responsibilities when possible. This will help you focus on what's most important and avoid burnout.

In addition to setting priorities and boundaries, it's important to take care of your physical, emotional, and mental health. Make time for exercise, healthy eating, relaxation, and self-care. These activities will help you recharge and stay energized for the things that matter most.

Another important aspect of balance is setting realistic goals and expectations for yourself. It's easy to get caught up in the idea of "having it all" or achieving unrealistic goals. However, this mindset can lead to disappointment, stress, and a lack of enthusiasm. Instead, focus on setting realistic goals that align with your priorities and values. Celebrate your progress and accomplishments, and learn from your setbacks and failures.

Finally, surround yourself with positive and supportive people who share your values and enthusiasm. Connect with like-minded individuals who can offer encouragement, advice, and support along your journey.

In summary, balance is crucial for fostering enthusiasm and achieving lasting success in every area of your being. Set priorities and boundaries, take care of your physical and emotional health, set realistic goals and expectations, and surround yourself with positive and supportive people. By creating balance in your life, you can unlock your full potential, overcome obstacles, and create a life you love.

33: How to Celebrate Successes to Boost Enthusiasm

When it comes to achieving our goals, we often focus on what we haven't yet accomplished, rather than celebrating our successes along the way. This can lead to a lack of enthusiasm and motivation, as we feel like we're not making progress or reaching our desired outcomes. However, celebrating successes is crucial for boosting enthusiasm and achieving lasting success in every area of your being.

So how do you celebrate successes in a way that boosts your enthusiasm and motivation? Here are some tips:

– Acknowledge your progress: Take time to reflect on the progress you've made towards your goals. Celebrate the milestones you've reached, no matter how small they may seem. Recognize the effort and dedication you've put into achieving your goals, and acknowledge the challenges you've overcome along the way.

– Share your successes with others: Don't be afraid to share your successes with friends, family, or colleagues. Celebrate your accomplishments with others and allow them to share in your joy and excitement. This can also help to inspire and motivate others to pursue their own goals.

– Reward yourself: Treat yourself to something special when you reach a milestone or achieve a goal. This could be as simple as taking a day off to relax and recharge, or as extravagant as planning a trip or buying a new piece of equipment. Whatever it is, make sure it aligns with your values and motivates you to keep pushing forward.

– Visualize your success: Take time to visualize yourself achieving your goals and experiencing the feelings of success and accomplishment. This can help to boost your enthusiasm and motivation, and keep you focused on your desired outcomes.

– Learn from your successes: Use your successes as an opportunity to learn and grow. Identify what worked well for you and what you can improve on in the future. This will help you to continually improve and achieve even greater success in the future.

Remember, celebrating your successes is not about being boastful or arrogant. It's about acknowledging your progress, rewarding yourself for your hard work, and boosting your enthusiasm and motivation. By celebrating your successes, you can create a positive cycle of growth and success in every area of your being.

In summary, celebrating your successes is crucial for boosting enthusiasm and achieving lasting success in every area of your being. Acknowledge your progress, share your successes with others, reward yourself, visualize your success, and learn from your successes. By celebrating your successes, you can create a positive cycle of growth and success in your life.

34: Overcoming Burnout to Ignite Enthusiasm

In today's fast-paced world, it's all too easy to become overwhelmed with work, personal obligations, and other stressors. When we're constantly on the go, it can be difficult to find the time and energy to pursue our passions and maintain our enthusiasm for life. This can lead to burnout, a state of emotional, physical, and mental exhaustion that can leave us feeling drained and uninspired. However, by taking steps to overcome burnout, we can reignite our enthusiasm and passion for life.

Here are some tips for overcoming burnout and reigniting your enthusiasm:

– Practice self-care: Take care of yourself physically, emotionally, and mentally. This means getting enough sleep, eating a healthy diet, exercising regularly, and engaging in activities that bring you joy and relaxation. When you prioritize self-care, you'll have more energy and motivation to pursue your passions.

– Set realistic goals: When we set unrealistic goals for ourselves, we can become overwhelmed and stressed. Instead, set goals that are achievable and aligned with your values. This will help you stay focused and motivated, and avoid burnout.

– Take breaks: It's important to take breaks throughout the day to recharge and refresh your mind. Whether it's taking a walk, meditating, or simply taking a few deep breaths, taking breaks can help you stay focused and productive.

– Create boundaries: Sometimes, we can become burned out because we take on too much and don't create boundaries for ourselves. Learn to say no to commitments that don't align with your values or priorities, and set limits for how much time you spend on work or other obligations.

– Seek support: Don't be afraid to seek support from friends, family, or a therapist if you're feeling overwhelmed or burnt out. Talking about your feelings and experiences can help you gain perspective and find solutions to your challenges.

– Reconnect with your passions: When we're burnt out, it's easy to lose sight of our passions and what brings us joy. Take time to reconnect with your passions and hobbies, whether it's reading, painting, or playing sports. This can help reignite your enthusiasm and remind you of what's important to you.

Remember, burnout is a natural part of life, but it doesn't have to be a permanent state. By taking steps to practice self-care, set realistic goals, take breaks, create boundaries, seek support, and reconnect with your passions, you can overcome burnout and reignite your enthusiasm for life.

In summary, burnout can leave us feeling drained and uninspired, but by taking steps to prioritize self-care, set realistic goals, take breaks, create boundaries, seek support, and reconnect with our passions, we can overcome burnout and reignite our enthusiasm for life. Don't let burnout hold you back from pursuing your passions and creating a life you love. Take care of yourself and find ways to reignite your inner spark.

35: How to Embrace Change for Enthusiasm

Change is inevitable in life, yet many of us resist it. We often cling to what is familiar and comfortable, even if it no longer serves us or brings us happiness. However, embracing change is essential if we want to ignite and maintain our enthusiasm for life. Here are some tips for embracing change and using it to fuel our enthusiasm:

– Embrace uncertainty: Change can bring uncertainty and fear of the unknown. However, it's important to embrace uncertainty and see it as an opportunity for growth and new experiences. When we let go of our need for control and embrace uncertainty, we open ourselves up to new possibilities and experiences.

– Focus on the positive: Change can also bring challenges and setbacks. However, it's important to focus on the positive aspects of change and the opportunities it presents. By focusing on the positive, we can maintain a positive attitude and outlook on life, which can help fuel our enthusiasm.

– Embrace new experiences: Change often brings new experiences, which can be exciting and energizing. Try new activities, explore new places, and meet new people. Embracing new experiences can help us break out of our comfort zone and ignite our enthusiasm for life.

– Learn from failure: Change can also bring failure and mistakes. However, it's important to learn from our failures and use them as opportunities for growth and learning. When we approach failure with a growth mindset, we can learn valuable lessons and use them to fuel our enthusiasm and success.

– Embrace challenges: Change often brings challenges and obstacles. However, it's important to embrace these challenges and see them as opportunities to grow and develop new skills. When we embrace challenges, we build resilience and confidence, which can help fuel our enthusiasm for life.

– Visualize your goals: Change can also be an opportunity to reassess our goals and priorities. Take time to visualize your goals and what you want to achieve in life. By visualizing your goals, you can stay focused and motivated, even in the face of change.

Remember, change is a natural part of life, and embracing it is essential if we want to ignite and maintain our enthusiasm for life. By embracing uncertainty, focusing on the positive, embracing new experiences, learning from failure, embracing challenges, and visualizing our goals, we can use change to fuel our enthusiasm and create a life we love.

In summary, change is inevitable in life, and embracing it is essential if we want to ignite and maintain our enthusiasm for life. By embracing uncertainty, focusing on the positive, embracing new experiences, learning from failure, embracing challenges, and visualizing our goals, we can use change to fuel our enthusiasm and create a life we love. Don't let fear of the unknown hold you back from pursuing your passions and embracing new opportunities. Embrace change and use it to fuel your inner spark.

36: Conclusion: Living Your Best Life with Enthusiasm

Enthusiasm is a powerful force that can transform your life in numerous ways. It can help you achieve your goals, overcome obstacles, and create a life that you love. But it's not always easy to maintain enthusiasm in the face of challenges, setbacks, and the stresses of daily life. That's why it's important to cultivate and nurture your enthusiasm on a regular basis.

Throughout this book, we've explored various strategies and techniques for igniting and maintaining enthusiasm in your life. We've talked about the importance of setting goals, creating a plan, and holding yourself accountable. We've discussed the role of balance, celebration, and gratitude in fostering enthusiasm. We've explored the dangers of burnout and the benefits of embracing change. And we've seen how enthusiasm can help you cultivate positive relationships, overcome adversity, and achieve lasting success.

Now it's time to bring all of these concepts together and put them into action. Here are some key takeaways to help you live your best life with enthusiasm:

36: CONCLUSION: LIVING YOUR BEST LIFE WITH EN-THUSIASM

– Set meaningful goals: Take time to reflect on what you truly want to achieve in your life. Create goals that align with your values and passions, and break them down into smaller, achievable steps.

– Create a plan: Once you have your goals in mind, create a detailed plan for achieving them. This plan should include specific actions, timelines, and measurable outcomes.

– Hold yourself accountable: Find ways to hold yourself accountable for your progress towards your goals. This could include setting deadlines, tracking your progress, or working with an accountability partner.

– Cultivate balance: Take care of your physical, emotional, and spiritual needs. Make time for activities that bring you joy, rest, and rejuvenation.

– Celebrate your successes: Take time to acknowledge and celebrate your accomplishments, no matter how small they may seem. This will help boost your confidence and keep you motivated.

– Avoid burnout: Recognize the signs of burnout and take

steps to prevent it. This may include taking breaks, delegating tasks, and setting boundaries.

– Embrace change: Instead of fearing change, see it as an opportunity for growth and learning. Embrace new experiences, take risks, and learn from your failures.

Remember, enthusiasm is a state of mind and a way of living. It's about being fully engaged in your life and finding joy and fulfillment in the journey. By incorporating the strategies and techniques we've explored in this book, you can unleash your inner spark and create a life that is filled with enthusiasm, purpose, and passion.

Thank You

As we reach the end of this book, I want to say thanks for reading this book.

I want to get this information out to as many people as possible. If you found this book helpful, I would greatly appreciate you leaving me a review. This helps others find the book as well.

Disclaimer

This document is geared towards providing exact and reliable information in regards to the topic and issue covered. The publication is sold on the idea that the publisher is not required to render an accounting, officially permitted, or otherwise, qualified services. If advice is necessary, legal, financial, medical or professional, a practiced individual in the profession should be ordered.

This information is not presented by a financial or medical practitioner and is for entertainment, educational and informational purposes only. The content is not intended as a substitute for professional medical advice, diagnosis, or treatment. Always seek the advice of your physician or other qualified health care provider with any questions you may have regarding a medical condition. Never disregard professional medical advice or delay in seeking it because of something you have read.

The information provided herein is stated to be truthful and consistent, in that any liability, in terms of inattention or otherwise, by any usage or abuse of any policies, processes, or directions contained within is the solitary and utter responsibility of the recipient reader. Under no circumstances

DISCLAIMER

will any legal responsibility or blame be held against the publisher for any reparation, damages, or monetary loss due to the information herein, either directly or indirectly.